Ford Motor Company

Manufacturers of Automobiles, Trucks and Tractors

Detroit, U.S.A.

TO ALL FORD DEALERS: May 25, 1927

As stated in our telegram to you we have released to the papers an official announcement of the new Ford car.

Attached is a copy of the complete announcement for your further information. UNDER NO CIRCUMSTANCES, are details of the new Ford car to be given out to anyone.

At the proper time you will be fully advised of all our plans for the public showing of this new car. At that time you will be given a complete plan of operation and schedule of our plans for cooperating with you.

Very truly yours,
FORD MOTOR COMPANY

W. A. Ryan
Manager of Sales

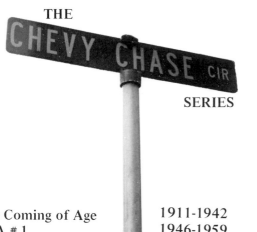

THE

SERIES

THE

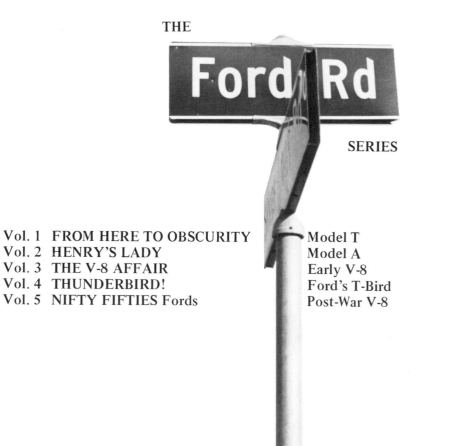

SERIES

FIRST PRINTING
November   1972
SIXTH PRINTING
June   1977

HENRY'S LADY

Model A

"An Illustrated History of the Model A Ford"

By **RAY MILLER**

with Photographs by **GLENN EMBREE**

THE EVERGREEN PRESS
Oceanside, California, 92054

HENRY'S Model A LADY

Library of Congress Catalog Card Number 72-77244
ISBN 0-913056-03-0

Printed by:

    Sierra Printers, Inc.
    Bakersfield, California

printed in U.S.A.

RAY MILLER, along with Bruce McCalley, another Founding Member of the Model T Ford Club of America, produced *FROM HERE TO OBSCURITY*, a book that has become the Standard Reference for those interested in the Model T Ford. From that effort, it was a relatively modest step to apply similar techniques of reporting to the pre-war Ford V-8, and the result was *THE V-8 AFFAIR*, which has already become the "bible" for those interested in the early "flathead" engine.

Ray has, in his younger days, owned many early Fords, and although he has in the past owned several Model A's, presently has limited his collection to an early Model T and a restored '36 Phaeton which he drives daily in nearby Oceanside, California, where he now makes his home.

In addition to having had the responsibility for the text and the production of this book, it was Ray who located the outstanding array of beautifully maintained cars used to illustrate this work. "Southern California's climate", says Ray, "peculiarly qualifies the area for this type of journal since so many well-restored cars are used here for so many days of the year.

GLENN EMBREE, well known to readers of *THE VINTAGE FORD*, served as President of the Model T Ford Club of America, and has provided the colorful covers for that magazine since its inception. Fundamentally a Photographic Essayist, Glenn has been involved with photography both as a hobby, and a Profession, since 1940.

Co-author, with Ray Miller, of *THE V-8 AFFAIR*, the illustrated history of the pre-war Ford V-8, Glenn has established an enviable pattern of photographic reporting which is continued in this book. Although his Studio, in Hollywood, California, is adorned with portraits of well-known celebrities, it is apparent that Glenn *enjoys* his automotive portraiture as the results exhibit an interest and excitement that would otherwise be lacking.

Glenn has had a long-continuing relationship with the Ford Motor Company, and with other nationally known organizations. His pictures are often used in well-received advertisements for products familiar to us all.

The Authors wish to thank those whose interest in this project was expressed by their encouragement and their cooperation. Needless to say, the owners of the featured cars are especially thanked, for, without their help, this Journal could never have been completed. In addition, we wish also to thank:

THE FORD MOTOR COMPANY for their permission to reproduce selected portions of their Model A Service Bulletins.

THE MODEL A RESTORERS CLUB OF ARIZONA who opened their Yuma Tour to our cameras in the Spring of 1972, and the **ORANGE COUNTY CHAPTER** of the **MODEL A FORD CLUB OF AMERICA** who did the same for us at their Pancake Breakfast in Santa Ana.

CARL BURNETT of Antique Automotive in San Diego, **HAROLD LOONEY,** of Vintage Auto Parts in Santa Ana, and **GENE VALDEZ** of Ford Parts Obsolete in Long Beach, all opened their vast inventories to our cameras, and Mr. Burnett received many telephone calls from the Author seeking correctly to resolve a confusion. To all of these gentlemen, we extend our thanks.

Especially to **ART EDWARDSON** of Phoenix do we extend our thanks for his permission for the use of his very perceptive sketches which add so much to the appearance of this book.

LES HENRY, of Dearborn, generously furnished information pertaining to production records reproduced elsewhere in this book, and offered his encouragement during a trip to San Diego on other matters.

BOB WHITE, of Fallbrook, California, aided in locating cars and correcting text, and, along with **AL COFFIELD,** of Phoenix, waded through the unpublished manuscript seeking to establish authenticity.

It remains for **RICHARD KRIST,** of Fullerton, California, to be acknowledged. In every journey, there is a first step, and it was Richard who initially provided us with an introduction to the wonderful people who welcomed our idea for this book.

In preparing this material, the authors have attempted to locate surviving unrestored original automobiles, where possible. Failing in this, we have employed, as models, restorations of the highest quality. Our gratitude is extended to the owners of these cars.

As is to be expected, there may well be items of incorrect date or style on any given automobile. Original cars may have been modified for any number of reasons by their owners; restorations are generally done to the best level of information available to the restorer, but occasionally a slip-up, sometimes of frightening proportions, will occur.

We have attempted to screen the inaccuracies; we hope that we may have succeeded in this attempt. This book was intended to be what it is, a copendium of information which will enable an observer to identify and to classify both cars and component parts. If there are errors, they are not to our knowledge.

The Authors

"A" FEW WORDS......

When the Author invited me to inspect his manuscript, I prepared myself to spend about an hour glancing through it. Three hours later, I was still at it, and I am certain that you readers will find it just as fascinating.

As a youngster, I first set eyes on a Model A Ford while visiting my dad's Ford dealership, the William A. White Motor Company. in Myrtle Creek, Oregon. Clearly I recall that at the time we had a maroon Model A Victoria with dealer's plates, and although Dad left the automobile business in 1933, a victim of the Depression, I have always retained an affection for the ubiquitous Model A Ford.

At the age of 15, I fell in love with a pristine 1931 Tudor Sedan which had been driven only about 10 miles a week by an elderly couple. Then, in 1947, I became the proud owner of a worn 1929 Coupe which was soon replaced by a rare 1931 Convertible Sedan, purchased for (believe it or not) $125 ! This car was my everyday transportation for seven years. Subsequent contact with the Model A Restorers Club resulted in my restoration of the A-400.

One thing led to another----- the car gained national publicity on a trip to Dearborn, Michigan, and years later, yours truly became one of the Founders of the Model A Ford Club of America.

At various times, I have owned six different Model A Fords, and many other cars including a 1935 Buick and a 1933 Auburn 8-105, but the Model A Ford still has a very special place in my life.

As to why, this book should provide some clues.

Bob White
Fallbrook, California
June 20, 1972

Mr. White is well known as a longtime Authority on the
Model A Ford. He is a Founding Member and past
Director of the MODEL A FORD CLUB OF AMERICA

It was Easter Week in 1939, and the busy New Castle ferry boat which plied between there and Pennsville, New Jersey, became the scene of the beginnings of this book. For, it was on that boat, in that long ago time, that I snapped this unusual photograph.

Then still a high school student with an early interest in automobiles not yet fully developed, I was on the traditional Easter Week journey to Washington, D.C., with family and friends when we spied an "old car". There was, however, a posture to that little standard Ford roadster that attracted us all.

Notably, while it also attracted the ferryman, it was ignored by his partner who appeared to believe that the old "jalopy" wasn't worth his attention. How little he knew! In the years to come, great numbers of people would savor such a moment, hoping all the while to locate such an unrestored automobile.

Had someone stolen the spare tire? Or, was an owner who was too unconcerned to replace a hub cap equally unaffected by his lack of a spare wheel? Perhaps these answers will never be known, but what *will* be set forth here is the result. some 33 years later, of an interest that has grown but never abated. An interest in the Model A Ford that began on the New Castle ferry and went on to produce . . . . .

HENRY'S LADY

In a Municipal Court in New York City, on January 10, 1928, sentence was suspended on Mr. L.T. Birch, who was the first man in the city to be arrested for speeding in the new Ford.

To Mr. Birch, we dedicate this book.

The Authors wish to give thanks to the Owners of cars featured in this work. No attempt has been made to isolate these cars, rather, since we have been endeavoring to describe the characteristics of a given year, we have deliberately employed those pictures which best served our immediate purpose. For this reason, adjacent photos may not necessarily show views of the same car.

CONTENTS

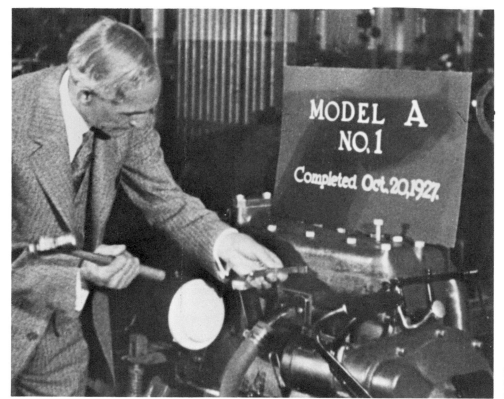

Photo courtesy of Ford Archives,
Henry Ford Musuem, Greenfield
Village, Dearborn, Michigan.

FORD MOTOR COMPANY

HISTORY: Incorporated under the laws of Michigan, June 16, 1903, and capitalized for $100,000, of which only $28,000 in cash was actually paid in. There were twelve stockholders, including Henry Ford, who held 25% of the stock. Later, in 1906, Mr. Ford acquired sufficient stock to bring his holdings up to 51%, and shortly thereafter purchased an additional 7½% This arrangement continued until 1919, when Edsel B. Ford, who had succeeded his father as president, purchased the remaining 41½% of outstanding stock. On July 9, 1919, the Ford Motor Co. was re-organized under the laws of Delaware, with an authorized capitalization of $100,000,000.

The company has thirty-six branches in the United States, of which thirty-three are assembly plants for the assembling of Ford cars and trucks, It has foreign offices and associate companies in South America, Cuba, Mexico, Europe, Egypt, and Japan. The Ford Motor Company of Canada, Ltd., (see appended statement) , located at Ford, Ontario, across the river from Detroit, supplies the trade in Canada and the British Empire, except the British Isles. Foreign plants, offices, or associated companies are located in Alexandria, Egypt; Antwerp, Belgium; Asnieres, Siene, France; Barcelona, Spain; Berlin, Germany; Buenos Aires, Argentina; Caracas, Venezuela; Copenhagen, Denmark; Cork, Ireland; Havana, Cuba; Helsingfors, Finland; Lima, Peru; Manchester, England; Mexico City, Mexico; Montevideo, Uraguay; Porte Alegre and Recife, Brazil; Stockholm, Sweden; Trieste, Italy, and Yokohama, Japan.

Company sold its first car in July, 1903, and during its first fiscal year produced 1,708 cars. During the first five years it built and sold approximately 25,000 Ford cars of various models, and on Oct. 1, 1908, produced the first Model T Ford car. It was seven years later, on December 10, 1915, when Model T Motor No. 1,000,000 was produced. Production rose rapidly after that, Model T No. 10,000,000 was produced June 4, 1924, and No. 15,000,000 on May 26, 1927.

Manufacture of the Model T car ceased with the production of No. 15,000,000, except for service parts to care for the repair requirements of approximately 9,000,000 Model T cars then in use.

Retooling of the Ford plants for the production of a new car, then already under way, began on a general scale, and on October 20, 1927, the first new Model A engine came off the engine assembly line at the Fordson plant and the same day was assembled into a new car. The new Model A car was formally announced to the public Nov. 26, 1927, and was given its first public showing on Dec. 2, 1927

1928 MOODY'S MANUAL OF INVESTMENTS pages 1554 & 1555

ther works have well documented the significance of Edsel Ford's contribution to the new Ford. Little can be added here to that which has been written about the elder Ford's stubborn clinging to the obsolescent Model T. Truly, it would appear that it was Edsel Ford who first accepted the need for the new car and then fought his father for his support in manufacturing it. Nevertheless, we cannot over-emphasise the contributions of the elder Ford, who, once having made his decision, persisted, at age 64, in designing and building what was for its time a most advanced new automobile.

From the Fords, both father and son, came a new vehicle so unlike the Model T that its very name came to suggest a rebirth and one which eclipsed the earlier Model A of 1903 to provide a whole new generation of people with an uncertainty as to *why* the Model A came *after* the Model T. "This new Ford", said the elder Ford, "must be the start of a new line", and so it was, for Model A has become the most heavily favored of *all* the automobiles now sought for restoration.

Photo courtesy of Ford Archives, Henry Ford Museum, Greenfield Village, Dearborn, Michigan

HENRY'S MADE A LADY OUT OF LIZZIE

Tune Ukulele

A D F♯ B

Put Capo on 1st fret

By WALTER O'KEEFE

Talk of this and talk of that,
Boys you must take off your hat,
HENRY'S MADE A LADY OUT OF LIZZIE!
Has she plenty, has she much?
Got the "tin" you love to touch,
HENRY'S MADE A LADY OUT OF LIZZIE!
They used to park her in a lot,
For that they charged two bits,
But now they charge you nothing,
And you park her at the Ritz.
She once had rattles in her wheel,
But now she's full of "sex-appeal",
HENRY'S MADE A LADY OUT OF LIZZIE!

Uke arr. by Joseph M. Weiss

3

"HENRY'S LADY"

The Model T Ford had been the butt of more jokes than possibly there were cars. For years, vaudeville comics made them laugh with "I don't need a speedometer, at 35 miles per hour, the engine falls out!", and "I had a Ford agency, but I couldn't compete with the five and ten cent store", and others too numerous to count.

Model T had been taken into the heart and bosom of Everyman, and "she" was treated like a family friend, a faithful servant, a loyal (if somewhat scatter-brained) employee. Affectionately, she had become, firstly, "tin Lizzie", and then "Lizzie" and thus she was to remain. Never a sight with which to be impressed, the stark, functional, unlovely lines of the Model T and the basic lack of creature comforts *earned* the never-changed appellation.

The "new Ford", introduced in December of 1928, changed all that though. With a rare eye for design, the very *appearance* of the car suggested character. It implied integrity, and promised performance. Incorporating a radically different sliding gear transmission, shock aborbers, twice the horsepower, and only a very slightly increased price, loyal Ford owners, without hesitation, "laid it on the line" and acquired the "new Ford".

Hours after driving the car for the first time, many were convinced that here at last was an automobile that not only "belonged", but which actually *led* the way to the future. No longer the butt of the comics' humor, the new Ford had joined the country club set, and in the words of a song written by Walter O'Keefe, and shortly to become immensely popular . . . .

"Henry Made a Lady Out of Lizzie"

The New York Times, the country's leading metropolitan daily newspaper, seems full of articles and stories relative to the Ford Motor Company, but among them are some which truly chronical the rapidly moving events surrounding the birth of the new Ford car. Following, by permission of the New York Times Company, is a partial index of these stories a study of which is most fascinating.

1926

September 4	EASTERN DISTRICT MANAGER ADVISED BY EDSEL FORD- NO NEW MODELS FOR 1927
December 15	NO NEW MODELS FOR 1927

1927

February 1	RUMORS OF PLAN TO PUT NEW TYPE CAR ON MARKET
March 17	PREPARATION OF NEW CAR REPORTED
March 18	WRITER IN DAILY METAL TRADE PREDICTS NEW TYPE FORD
April 7	RUMORS OF NEW GEARSHIFT CARS
May 19	SPOKESMAN FOR FORD DENIES RUMORS THAT NEW DESIGN IS TO BE PUT ON MARKET
May 22	FINAL DESIGN REPORTED TO BE "UNCOMPLETE"
May 26	OFFICIALS ANNOUNCE NEW THREE-SPEED CAR WILL BE PRODUCED
May 27	15,000,000TH MODEL T CAR PRODUCED
June 5	ANNOUNCEMENT OF NEW MODEL HURTING SALE OF T TYPE
June 9	EXTENSIVE NEW CAMPAIGN TO PROMOTE NEW CAR PLANNED
June 12	REPORT OF PLANS FOR NEW CAR
June 19	ASSEMBLY PLANT AT MASSACHUSETTS TO MAKE READY FOR NEW MODEL
June 22	REPORT, SAID TO BE AUTHENTIC, GIVES DETAILS; EDSEL FORD DENIES AUTHENTICITY
June 23	DESCRIPTION CALLED FICTIOUS
June 26	FEATURE ARTICLE BY T.C.YOUNG ON HENRY FORD NOTES CHANGES NECESSITATED BY PRODUCTION OF NEW CAR
August 12	HENRY FORD HAS FIRST FLIGHT IN SPIRIT OF ST LOUIS WITH LINDBERGH EDSEL IS SPIRIT'S SECOND PASSENGER
July 31	AT 64, HENRY FORD FACES HIS BIGGEST JOB WITH NEW CAR
July 31	HENRY FORD DISCUSSES NEW CAR
August 11	EDSEL FORD MAKES STATEMENT
August 23	NEW TRUCK TYPE TO BE PRODUCED

October 11	RUSH OF ADVANCE ORDERS REPORTED
October 16	FORD AGENCIES (DEALERS) WAITING
October 23	FIRST MODEL A TURNED OUT
October 26	NOT OKAYED FOR PRODUCTION
October 30	PUBLIC AWAITS IT
November 2	FIRST ONE RUN OFF ASSEMBLY LINE, BEING TESTED BY HENRY FORD
November 30	DEALERS SWAMPED BY INQUIRIES
December 1	PRICES, DEMOS, AT DETROIT; PRODUCTION PLANS
December 2	EXHIBITED AT NEW YORK CITY
December 3	SHOWN IN LONDON
December 7	CROWDS VIEW CAR IN NYC SHOWROOM
December 9	RESIDENTS OF SUFFOLK & NASSAU COUNTIES CHARTER BUSSES TO VIEW DISPLAY IN NYC
December 14	SENATOR COUSENS PRESENTED WITH ONE THOMAS EDISON INSPECTS ONE
December 23	WILL ROGERS PRESENTED WITH ONE

1928

January 8	THEFT INSURANCE RATES QUESTIONED
January 10	QUESTION OF BRAKES RAISED IN WASHINGTON' AND PENNSYLVANIA; COMPANY OFFICIALS SAY THEY WILL CONFORM TO REQUIREMENTS
January 18	WILL BE EQUIPPED WITH ANOTHER BRAKE
February 13	OPERATION REFUSED IN GERMANY BECAUSE OF BRAKES
February 21	NYC HOLDERS OF DRIVERS LICENSE FOR OLD MODELS WILL NOT BE REQUIRED TO TAKE NEW TEST FOR NEW MODEL
February 26	ENJOINED IN GERMANY BECAUSE OF BRAKES
March 11	GERMAN COURT RESCINDS INJUNCTION
March 23	INSURANCE RATES ON NEW MODEL SAID LOWER
May 4	EDSEL FORD ANNOUNCES NEW TIME-PAYMENT PLAN
May 20	PRODUCTION GOAL 5000 CARS PER DAY
June 14	FORDOR SEDAN UNDER WAY
August 23	NOW ABOUT 300,000 OWNERS OF NEW FORDS
November 14	NEW WORKS PLANNED FOR DAGENHAM, ENGLAND

Photo courtesy of Ford Archives, Henry Ford Museum, Dearborn, Michigan

1929

January 5	PLANS FOR PRIVATE SHOWING IN NEW YORK
January 6	TOWN SEDAN, CABRIOLET, & STATION WAGON ON DISPLAY
January 27	TAXICABS MUST SEAT FIVE TO BE LEGAL IN NEW YORK
March 17	MODEL A CARS REACH NEW RECORD; 8000/DAY
May 17	EDSEL FORD TURNS FIRST SOD FOR NEW PLANT IN DEGENHAM , ENGLAND AND BENDS SPADE
May 21	NEW MODEL A FORDOR SEDAN IN PRODUCTION
May 28	KEARNEY (N.J.) PLANT SOLD TO WESTERN ELECTRIC
June 6	HENRY FORD RECEIVES ONE OF THE FIRST THREE EDISON JUBILEE STAMPS
June 7	HENRY FORD BORROWED TWO CENTS TO PAY FOR THE STAMP
June 13	APPLIES TO POLICE COMMISSION FOR PERMISSION TO SUPPLY FLEET OF TAXICABS FOR OPERATION IN NEW YORK CITY
June 30	NEW PRODUCTION RECORD REACHED — 9100 CARS & TRUCKS/ DAY
July 14	NEW TWO-WINDOW FORDOR SEDAN IN PRODUCTION
July 24	2,000,000 MODEL A'S COMPLETED
July 31	NEW JERSEY MAN'S 58,850 PENNIES, SAVED IN 4 YEARS BUY FORD
October 3	RUMORS OF SHUT-DOWN TO CHANGE MODELS DENIED
November 1	PRICE CUTS ANNOUNCED; INTENDED TO HELP DISPOSE OF HEAVY STOCKS
November 19	RUMORS OF NEW MODELS REVIVED
November 21	DENVER PLANT VIRTUALLY CLOSED TO ALLOW DEALERS TO DISPOSE OF OVERSTOCK
November 23	ALL ASSEMBLY PLANTS IN U.S. OUTSIDE OF DETROIT TO CLOSE FOR READJUSTMENT
December 29	NEW MODEL A DESCRIBED
December 31	NEW MODELS ON MODEL A CHASSIS DESCRIBED

1930

January 1	NEW MODEL DISPLAYED IN NEW YORK CITY
January 7	DEALERS REPORT 250,000 VISITORS SEE NEW MODEL IN NEW YORK
January 26	NEW STEEL ALLOY USED
February 9	NEW FEATURES OF THE MODEL A
February 23	NEW MODEL AA TRUCK CHASSIS
April 27	NEW MODEL A DELUXE COUPE
June 22	NEW DELUXE PHAETON
August 31	NEW DELUXE ROADSTER
December 14	VICTORIA ANNOUNCED
December 21	LETTER TO DEALERS DENIES RUMOR MODEL A IS TO BE REPLACED

1931

January 2	PRICES REDUCED
January 3	ANNUAL SHOW AT DETROIT: NO RADICAL CHANGES IN MODEL A
February 13	LUXFORD TAXICAB COMPANY ANNOUNCES 15 & 5 CENT RATE TO BEGIN OPERATION IN NEW YORK WITH FORD TAXICABS
February 25	SIX FORD CABS LICENSED AT STANDARD RATES
April 12	NEW TOWN SEDAN INTRODUCED
April 15	PLANS TO PLACE CAR NO. 20,000,000 IN MUSEUM AFTER TOUR OF COUNTRY
May 24	NEW STANDARD SEDAN INTRODUCED
June 12	PROPOSED NEW CAR TO HAVE LONGER WHEELBASE & 8-CYLINDER ENGINE
July 30	SHUT-DOWN OF ALL PLANTS SCHEDULED FOR AUGUST 1ST; 75,000 OUT OF WORK

1932

March 31	INTRODUCTION OF THE NEW MODEL V-8 FORD

Try to get a perspective. The Ford Motor Company had been producing its Model T since 1908. For almost 20 years, the car had been relatively unchanged. True, there *were* literally

thousands of fairly small changes, and the net result was a car that looked quite unlike the first one, but fundamentally, the Model T Ford had never really changed.

By 1927, those around him, including, of course, his son Edsel, had finally persuaded Henry Ford to abandon his beloved Model T and to produce an entirely new car, one which would return the Ford Motor Company to a competitive position.

Think of it this way. Suppose that Volkswagon, in 1972, after producing over 15,000,000 of their little "beetle" since 1949, should suddenly feel its competition creeping up on it and announce a decision to cease production of their little "bug" and manufacture a new car with a turbine engine, compressed air starter, and concentric cone transmission! The effect on the Market would be startling. Their competition would be alarmed, and millions of loyal VW owners would eagerly await the coming of the "new Volkswagon".

That is about the way that it was in late 1927, and the "new Ford", to be shown in New York City on December 2, 1927, was not yet known as the "Model A". Neither was it referred to as the "1928 model", as Ford was at the moment still offering the last of the Model T line of cars. In 1927, the planned-obsolescence theory of Merchandising had not yet been refined, and the cos-

metic face-lifting mechanism for selling cars had not yet been developed. As a result, the car then introduced, was offered simply as the "new Ford".

The 1928 "NEW FORD"

Ford Motor Company

Manufacturers of Automobiles, Trucks and Tractors

LOS ANGELES, CAL.

IN REPLYING REFER TO

1

December 1, 1927

TO ALL DEALERS:

This is to confirm telegram of even date giving you the LIST PRICES, F O B Detroit, on the new Ford Car:

Phaeton	$395.00
Roadster	385.00
Chassis	325.00
Coupe	495.00
Sport Coupe with Rumble) Seat as standard equip-) ment)	550.00
Tudor Sedan	495.00
Fordor Sedan	570.00
Commercial Pick-up	395.00
1 1/2 Ton Truck Chassis) complete with starter) as standard equipment)	460.00
Truck Cab	85.00
Express Body	55.00
Stake Body	65.00
Platform Body	50.00
Bumpers , front and rear	15.00 per set extra

Spare wire wheel standard equipment on all cars and trucks. Extra price on Dual High Truck Equipment to be announced later.

From the above you will note that we will have a separate Pick-Up Type in our line of Commercial Cars.

Discount to Dealers on the Detroit List Price remains the same, i.e. 20%.

Yours truly

FORD MOTOR COMPANY

J. H. Banek

Branch Manager

JWC KBG

On December 1, 1927, the Los Angeles, California, Offices of the Ford Motor Company advised its Dealers by telegram of the List Prices of the new Ford car. A copy of that telegram was later sent in the form of the above confirming letter.

World Startled By False Rumor of Mussolini's Death

The Weather
CLOUDY TONIGHT AND FRIDAY

Springfield Daily News

LARGEST EVENING CIRCULATION 2c

48th YEAR, NO. 170 | Established in 1880 By CHARLES J. BELLAMY | SPRINGFIELD, MASS.: THURSDAY EVENING, DECEMBER 1, 1927 | TWENTY-EIGHT PAGES

FORD AUTO WAR HITS STOCK MARKET

HERE AT LAST --- HENRY FORD'S NEW CARS WHICH HAVE STARTLED THE AUTOMOTIVE WORLD

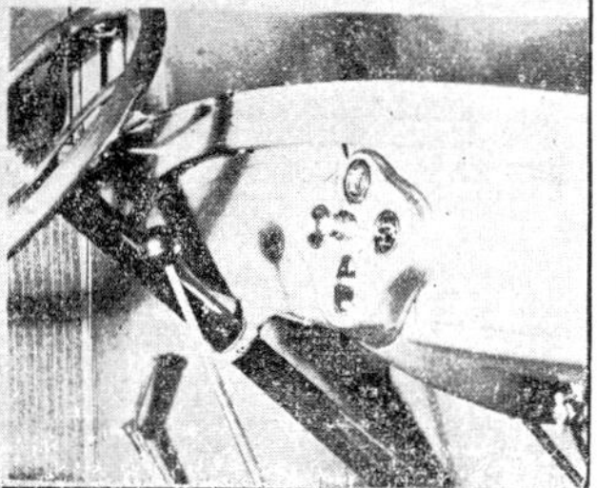

Photo on the left shows the new Ford coupe which, with other models will be placed on public display tomorrow. On the extreme right is the new sport roadster, with the rumble seat optional in this model. In center panel, upper left, the new phaeton; upper right, the Tudor sedan, long, low and roomy with graceful lines; lower left, the four-passenger sport coupe, and lower right, the interior of the new Ford car, showing instrument panel, steering wheel with lighting switch in the center and the gear shift hand lever.

Clarence Chamberlin Here for Conference on Airplane Motor Factory

Man Who Flew to Germany "To Get a Glass of Beer" Discusses Project With Vice-President Hillman of Chamber of Commerce; May Return Again to Meet City's Financial Leaders

May Locate Airplane Plant in Springfield

CLARENCE D. CHAMBERLIN

Clarence D. Chamberlin, noted transatlantic flyer who piloted the "Columbia" to Germany, "to get a glass of beer," was in brief conference here this morning with F. J. Hillman, executive vice-president of the Chamber of Commerce. Chamberlin has been making a survey of New England manufacturing cities for sites to set up a factory to manufacture airplane parts pending his entry into the airplane transport and air "flivver" fields. He came here from Hartford where yesterday he was tendered a large reception and banquet and where also inducements were made to have him locate his factory for manufacturing his plane motors.

At the conference here today with Hillman, preliminary steps were taken to have the noted flyer seriously consider what Springfield has to offer with respect to location of his factory here.

Springfield's transportation facilities, distribution center possibilities, existing sites, financial resources, supply of highly skilled labor, and other industrial and commercial assets were sketched by Hillman to Chamberlain.

The local Chamber of Commerce official also arranged for the trans-Atlantic pilot to meet certain financial leaders of the city for conference as well as inspection of local sites suitable for his proposed plant. The conference, it is thought, will mean that Chamberlain will visit Springfield again before he completes his survey of New England for sites for his airplane factory.

Motor Factory to be Somewhere In New England

At Hartford yesterday Chamberlain stated that his motor factory will be located in New England with the ships themselves being built in the Middle West. He said definite decision on the site was to be made this month, for it is planned to make deliveries by next spring.

Chamberlain indicated that his firm would engage in manufacture of "air flivvers," enter the air transport field through a liason with railroads and steamship lines, which would serve as auxiliaries to their regular services, and organize a chain of aviation schools, from which pilots with preliminary training would be graduated as assistant pilots on the air lines planes.

Inasmuch as Chamberlain indicated that it was unnecessary that the factory site adjoin a flying field, Springfield's chances of consideration, it is thought, may be more than fair.

The visit of the transatlantic flyer here was carefully guarded from the public and the local Chamber of Commerce official said he was bound by strict confidence not to divulge Chambelain's destination after his brief stopover in Springfield.

DRIVES CAR UP ONE MILE CLIMB TO THE SUMMIT OF MOUNT TOM

Ralph Mulford Noted Racer and Hill Climber, Is First to Make Trip

Holyoke, Dec. 1—History was made on Mount Tom this morning when Ralph Mulford of Cleveland, O., famous automobile race and hill climber, drove a Chandler de luxe touring car up the one-mile incline to the Summit house. It was the first time that such a feat was attempted and while the difficult ascent was made it was a tedious affair owing to the fact that the cable track disallowed sufficient clearance for the axle and cleated planks had to be laid along the ties.

Mulford is well known in the automobile world, having driven a machine to the top of Pike's peak in 1921, a nine-mile climb with a 28 per cent grade, and also to the top of Mount Washington, in California. There are three separate grades on the local mountain, seven, 14, and 21 per cent, respectively.

The climb today was made possible through the Laporte Motor company, under whose auspices the arrangements were made and through the courtesy of the Mount Tom railway. Moving pictures were made including closeups of Mulford, M. Albert Laporte, and his business associate, Ralph Burnham, both of Springfield.

The descent proved to be les thrilling than anticipated but was completed this afternoon after Mr Mulford had driven the famous car around the top of the famous mountain.

FAVORS RED PEPPER IN FIGHTING YEGGS

Chicago, Dec. 1—Lesson No 2 on "How to foil bandits," was given the women of Chicago today by Chief of Detectives William E. O'Connor. It advised women to carry a package of red peper to be hurled into the cases of morons and would-be holdup men.

"Throw the pepper and then scream as loud as you can," said the chief.

Lesson No 1 told residents to leave a light burning when they go out for an evening, thus making it appear to would-be housebreakers that some one is at home.

UKRANIANS IN SHARP REVOLT, LATEST REPORT

More Than 5000 People Killed Word Heard in Bucharest

Bucharest, Dec. 1 — Reports of a widespread Ukrainian revolt, which was put down after lasting three months and resulting in the deaths of more than 5000 people, were disparaged here today.

The Rumanian foreign office was without any information of such a re- that small revolts in Ukraine were continuing, but were restricted to local street skirmishes. Even the Russian monarchist circles doubted the seriousness of the revolt.

Fall River, Dec. 1—William P. J. Perry was held here today in connection with the death of Roger Jean, six, who was' struck and killed by Perry's automobile on Pleasant street last night. Perry was charged with reckless driving.

MARRIAGE BAR TO THE WOMEN AS TEACHERS IN CHICOPEE

School Committee Will Appoint No M re of Them in the Day School

Chicopee, Dec. 1—At the meeting of the school committee last evening it was voted to adopt the following amendment to the general laws governing school regulations to chapter 4, section1:—

"No women who are married shall be elected to permanent positions as teachers in the day schools. Married women may be appointed only on a substitute basis by the superintendent with the consent of the school committee; they shall not receive election from the school committee, nor shall they be eligible for tenure. Teachers who marry after entering the service shall present their resignations, to be effective at once."

This action by the school committee will not come as a surprise to Chicopee people, as the question of married teachers being retained in the employment of the school department has been discussed widely. This step by the Chicopee board is not the first taken along these lines as a number of other cities are now abiding by this ruling of the general laws governing the school body.

In fact, most of the citizens approve of this measure as the consensus appears to be that when a teacher is married she should sacrifice her position as a teacher and give the opportunity to the unemployed who have trained for such positions. Any present teacher who is married and served the necessary amount of time for temporary appointment will find that election as a permanent teacher is now impossible through this new ruling. Those married teachers who are now permanent teachers will not be affected by this new measure.

The same idea of municipal employment was brought up before the board of aldermen, but when it was requested that all those in the employ of city government resign from their positions the proposal was squelched.

TWO FIREMEN INJURED AS TRUCK HITS TREE

Peabody, Dec. 1—Two firemen were in a hospital here today as result of injuries received last night when a fire truck skidded and hit a tree. Those hurt were Capt William Costello and Driver John Barrett.

FEMALE "HUSBAND" GOES TO JAIL

Boston—Ethel Kimbal, who recently lived for two years as the "husband" of another woman, today began a 10½ months' jail term, imposed for the larceny of $47.

Beach Confessed Murder To Him, Witness Says as State Plays Trump Card

Samuel Bark Declares on Stand That Poultry Fancier, Accused With Mrs Lilliendahl, Asked for Money to Help His Defense; Plea for Cash Came During Talk in Baltimore

Court House, Mays Landing, N. J., Dec. 1—Willis Beach, 50-year-old alleged lover of Mrs Margetr Lilliendahl, and jointly accused with her of murdering her husband, confessed to Samuel Bark, in Baltimore, shortly after the slaying, that he had fired the fatal shot, Bark testified today.

In Bark's testimony, at the opening of the fourth day's session this morning, the state had played its ace.

For three days dozens of witnesses have marched off and on the stand amidst a maze of questioning designed to pin the murder on Mrs Lilliendahl and Beach by a net of circumstantial evidence, but not until Bark's appearance on the stand today did the state definitely link Beach with the killing.

Needed Some Money

Bark plunged immediately into the high spots of his testimony. After stating that his home is in Texas but that he was temporarily stopping in Baltimore, Bark declared that Beach had come to him and admitted that he had shot the doctor and needed money to get "out of the jam."

The questions by Assistant Prosecutor Hinkle, and Barks' answers follow:—

Q.—How long have you known Beach?

A.—A year.

Q.—Did you see Beach in a Baltimore park in September? (The murder occurred September 15.)

A.—Yes.

Q.—What did he say to him?

A.—There was a man named Thompson with me and I said to Beach I see by the paper they want

Continued on Page Twenty-four

MUSSOLINI AT HIS DESK AFTER DEATH RUMOR

World Aroused by Report That Originates on Berlin Market

Rome, Dec. 1—Premier Mussolini was in the best of health today. Rumors circulated in Berlin that he had been assassinated were branded officially as "inventions."

Berlin, Dec. 1—A rumor, denounced from Rome as false, that Premier Benito Mussolini had been assassinated, was believed today to have been a Bourse manouver designed to cause a fall in the value of Italian currency.

It is thought that Vienna exchange rate speculators started the rumor, which soon reached newspapers here and caused urgent queries to be sent to Rome from all over the world.

That the rumors had effect was shown by the opening quotations on the London money market. The rate to the pound sterling for the Italian lire was 90.20 compared with 89.825 at last night's closing.

British government officials regarded the rumor as false. No intimation of an attack upon the Italian statesman was received through official channels from Rome.

Portland—Fifteen hunters lost their lives and many others were wounded during Maine's hunting season, which ended at midnight.

AGED VETERAN DROPS DEAD AT RELIEF BUREAU

Sylvester Pendleton, 84, Civil War Soldier, Dies at City Hall

Sylvester Pendleton, 84, Civil war veteran, of 52 Huntington street, subject to heart attacks, died suddenly at relief bureau. Pendleton was walking along Pynchon street when he became severely ill and asked a passerby to take him to the soliers' relief office where his record as a Civil war veteran was on file. The unknown Samaritan quit the office immediately after assisting Mr Pendleton there. Maj Roberts of the soldiers' relief bureau immediately got in communication with Mrs W. A. R. Chapin and Walter E. Jackson, city and assistant city physicians, respectively, but before medical aid arrived Mr Pendleton arrived. Medical Examiner Dr Frederick Jones was then summoned and pronounced death due to heart failure.

Pendleton was born in New York city, March 26, 1942. On August 22, 1861, he enlisted with the northern forces, in the Civil war, with Co K, 3d New York infantry. His military service ran through the greater period of the war, his honorable discharge coming on August 22, 1865.

Mr Pendleton has made his home here generally since 1910. Previous to that time he lived in Westfield and

Continued on Page Twenty-four

FORMER YALE STAR HELD FOR GRAND JURY IN SHOOTING CASE

Gilbert Stanley's Bail Raised to $20,000 and Furnished at Great Barrington

(Special Dispatch to The Daily News)

Great Barrington, Dec. 1—Gilbert Stanley of Sheffield and this town pleaded not guilty before Judge Walter B. Sanford in district court today, to a charge of manslaughter in connection with the death of Peter Fulco last Saturday night and was bound over to the grand jury which will come in the second Monday in January at Pittsfield.

The warrant was read by Clerk Dennis C. Killeen. The defendant, who was graduated from Yale in 1919, and was a famous hockey star during his years in college, was represented by Attys Frederick M. Myers and Thomas F. Cassidy of Pittsfield. The commonwealth was represented by State Detective David J. Manning of Springfield, Asst-Dist Atty Charles H. Wright of Pittsfield being out of town. No evidence was presented on either side.

Lieut Manning asked that bonds which were fixed at $10,000 by Judge Sanford on Sunday be raised to $20,000 and this was ordered by the court. The bail was furnished by John H. C. Church and Charles M. Gibbs. The courtroom was crowded to capacity, among those in the audience being Headmaster Seaver M. Buck of the Berkshire school, where Stanley is manager and on whose grounds the alleged crime took place, several members of the faculty and two of Stanley's brothers.

The cases of Mrs Mabel St James and Michael J. Cleary, Jr., who were in Fulco's party on Saturday night, were continued for two weeks. They are charged with disturbing the peace and drunkenness.

FOUR KILLED WHEN ERIE TRAIN HITS CAR

Automobile Was Carrying Employes of General Electric Co's Decatur Plant

Decatur, Ind., Dec. 1—Four persons were killed here today when their automobile was struck by an Erie railroad freight train at a crossing. The dead:—

Alfred Stuttler, 36; Hazel Lummon, 24; Mrs Kenneth Hoblet, 23, and Hobart Strickler, 33. All four were employed in the Decatur plant of the General Electric company.

Barnstable—Fog caused postponement of a trial here when it prevented Aircraft Inspector Robert L. O'Brien, a witness, from flying from Boston to Barnstable.

General Motors Issues Slump as New Car Appears

Hand of Auto Magnate Felt in Wall Street on Eve of Public Demonstration of Late Ford Models; Cities Throughout Nation Will be Scene of Displays Tomorrow; Action Comes as Ford's Reply to His Competitors

New York, Dec. 1—The hand of Henry Ford was felt in Wall street today. Publication of the price list of the new Ford car, to be shown to the public tomorrow for the first time, reacted on motor shares and brought sharp declines in prices to many important issues.

General Motors, Ford's main competitor, suffered the heaviest losses. Opening at 130¼, up ½ point from yesterday's close, it dropped to 128½ during the first hour of trading, recovering a little later to 129.

Ford is ready today to strike back at those leaders in the automotive industry who have been making inroads upon his status as the nation's automobile "king." Tomorrow the new Ford cars will go on display throughout the country and in them is the Dearborn genius's answer to those who seek to usurp his "throne." In a well-advertised and well-timed campaign, Mr Ford has startled the automobile world as he promised he would some six months ago.

Rumors of a finish fight between Ford and General Motors gains credence with appearance of the new Ford models. Obvioously far superior to the old cars, the new types are lower in price, all things considered, than the model T. In this price slashing is seen a challenge to those who have entered the low-priced field in an effort to dim the powers of Henry Ford.

Big Reception Due

It is announced that but 500 of the new cars are now available and these will be used in the displays which open tomorrow. Speeding up of production is regarded as only a matter of days, and the Ford company has promised that deliveries will start in January. Meantime in many cities where the new Fords will be shown tomorrow civic programs have been arranged that might do honor to the visit of a foreign monarch.

New Model Tested

A model of the new car was shown to newspaper men at the Dearborn laboratories today.

Through blinding eddies of snow and over rutty roads, rim deep in mud, the car was driven at 62 miles an hour, twirled about, brought to abrupt stops and taken around curves at a breath taking pace.

The demonstration made one forget that the new car differed from the old in having the standard gear shift, four wheel brakes, a greater capacity for speed, hydraulic shock absorbers, steel spoke wheels and in 100 other unseen ways, and resolved itself into an unanswered puzzle as to what magic of balance kept the car from tipping over or plunging into the ditch.

Edsel Ford, after the demonstration, answered questions. Among other statements he made were these:—

1. The company hopes to reach a production of 1000 cars a day in January and step up production 1000 monthly, that is 1000 a day in January, 2000 a day in February, 3000 a day in March, and so on.

Deliveries in January

2. The company will continue to make parts for the old cars, or which it is estimated there are some 10,000,000 in operation, just as long as there is a demand for replacement parts.

3. Only about 550 of the new cars have been built and the probability is that there will be no deliveries to prospective buyers until some time in January.

4. The cars of smaller bore will be manufactured for the French and English trade to meet the resistance of the high horsepower tax in those countries.

5. The assembly line will be at the Rouge plant. Work at the Highland Park plant will be confined largely to radiators, steering gear, front and rear axles, fabric and batteries.

6. The working force at Highland Park, now between 30,000 and 35,000, has moved upward from its low and will continue to increase weekly from now on.

Statement by Company

A formal statement issued by the company reads:—

"Six months ago Henry Ford announced the coming production of a new Ford car, superior in design and

Continued on Page Twenty-four

Prices Regarded as Lower Than Those On the Old Model

Detroit, Mich., Dec. 1—The Ford Motor company has announced the prices of the various models of the new motor car which Henry Ford has built to take the place of the car which made him known throughout the world and for which in return the world made him one of its richest men.

The new price list, in comparison with that of the old Model T, follows:—

Prices of the Model A cars, F. O. B. Detroit, as compared with prevailing prices for Model T are as follows:—

Type	Model A.	Model T.
Tudor sedan	$495	$495
Fordor sedan	570	545
Coupe	495	485
Sport coupe	550	...
*Phaeton	395	380
Roadster	385	350
Roadster with pickup	395	381
Chassis	325	300
TRUCKS		
Truck and chassis	460	375
Truck chassis with cab	515	460
Truck chassis with cab and stake body	610	525
Truck chassis with cab and platform body	595	525

*Corresponding Model T touring car type. No comparison is possible on the sport coupe, as this is a new type.

The prices are read by automobile experts as constituting a reduction nearly all along the line. Where there are increases, improvements in the product and the sum of additional equipment are believed to more than balance the advance and give a margin in favor of those who consider the new prices a saving over the old.

DAWES OUT OF WHITE HOUSE RACE, HE SAYS

Disavows Candidacy in Formal Statement at Washington

Washington, Dec. 1—Standing beneath the roof of the White House executive offices, Vice-President Dawes today indorsed ex-Gov Frank O. Lowden for the 1928 Republican presidential nomination. Dawes stated that he was not a candidate for the nomination.

His statement, dictated to the White House stenographer, who takes President Coolidge's dictation, was issued after Dawes had called upon the President to pay his respects.

The Vice-President would not comment upon the President's "I do not choose to run" statement.

Amesbury—Mrs Bessie Zeihler, 40, mother of 13 children, sacrificed her life in an attempt to rescue one of her children from a well. Later the child was saved.

NEW FORD TUDOR SEDAN

An example of the fine coachwork of the new Ford cars. New military-type sun visor and crown roof. Narrow pillars and new door construction give unusual vision. Both front seats fold forward, giving easy access to rear seat. Ample space between seats. Your choice of four artistic color harmonies—an unusual feature in a low-price car.

$495
(F. O. B. Detroit)

First Pictures of the New Ford Car

Get complete details TOMORROW at Ford salesrooms

FOR SEVERAL years we have been working on the new Ford car. For weeks and months you have been hearing rumors about it. For the past few days you have been reading some of the details of it in the newspapers.

Whatever you do tomorrow, take at least fifteen minutes to get the full story of this new automobile.

You will realize then that it is an entirely new and different Ford car, designed and created to meet modern conditions —a car that brings you more beauty, speed, quiet, comfort, safety, economy and stamina than you ever thought possible in a low-price car.

Automobile history will be made tomorrow, for the new Ford is not only new in appearance and performance . . . it is new in mechanical design. Many features of it are exclusive Ford developments. Some are wholly new in automobile practice. Its low price is a reflection of manufacturing improvements and economies that are as epoch-making as the car itself.

Nineteen years of experience in building 15,000,000 automobiles are behind the new Ford car and have counted in its making. Resources unmatched in the motor car industry are its heritage and its birthright.

The Ford policy of owning the source of raw materials, of making virtually every part, of doing business at a small profit per car, has cut many dollars off the price you would ordinarily have to pay for a car like this.

So we say to you—learn about this new Ford car tomorrow. Compare it with any other car in the light-car field for beauty of line—for comfort—for speed

—for quick acceleration—for flexibility in traffic . . . for steadiness at all speeds . . . for power on the hills . . . for economy and low cost of up-keep . . . for its sturdy ability to stand up under countless thousands of miles of service.

Then you will know why tomorrow will be remembered as one of the greatest days in the entire history of the automobile industry. . . . Then you will know why the new Ford car will be *your* car.

NOTE THESE FEATURES

Beautiful new low body lines

Choice of four colors

55 to 65 miles an hour

Remarkable acceleration

40 horse-power

Four-wheel brakes

Standard, selective gear shift

Hydraulic shock absorbers

20 to 30 miles per gallon of gasoline

Theft-proof coincidental lock

Typical Ford economy and reliability

STANDARD EQUIPMENT ON ALL NEW FORD CARS

Starter	Dashlight
Five steel-spoke wheels	Mirror
Windshield wiper	Rear and stop light
Speedometer	Oil gauge
Gasoline gauge	Tools
Pressure grease gun lubrication	

© 1927, Ford Motor Company

NEW FORDOR SEDAN

A big roomy car. Wide seats. Generous leg-room front and rear. Four convenient doors. Unusually large windows. Rich upholstery and full-nickeled hardware. Dome light. Your choice of four artistic colors.

$570
(F. O. B. Detroit)

NEW FORD ROADSTER

A long, low, chummy car. As fast as it looks. Wide doors. Deep cushions. Rich upholstery. Full-nickeled hardware. Rumble seat optional. Your choice of four beautiful color harmonies.

$385
(F. O. B. Detroit)

NEW FORD COUPE

There is a bit of the European touch in the coachwork and contour of this new Ford Coupe. Handy package shelf in back of seat and unusually large waterproof luggage space in rear deck. Your choice of four beautiful colors.

$495
(F. O. B. Detroit)

NEW FORD SPORT COUPE

Combines the alert smartness of the roadster and the advantages of a closed car. Rumble seat standard. Landau irons on rear quarter. Finished in four artistic color harmonies.

$550
(F. O. B. Detroit)

NEW FORD PHAETON

Another long, low, roomy car. All four doors open forward. Curtains open and close with doors. Side curtains have unusually large windows. Your choice of four artistic colors.

$395
(F. O. B. Detroit)

FORD MOTOR COMPANY
Detroit, Michigan

IDENTIFYING MODELS BY YEAR

Before proceeding to a pictorial essay on the Model A Ford, it will be well to study these preliminary photographs. It is the intent of the Authors to provide the reader here with a set of guidelines by which he can make his own subsequent determinations of the particular "model year" of a given automobile.

Although changing frequently in both minor and in major areas, the Model A, like its predecessor, the Model T, shared a commonality throughout its production life. Certainly there were many parts which did not interchange, but there were far more that did, and so, in a sense, and with apologies to Gertrude Stein, "a Model A is a Model A, is a Model A".

There *were* however, small, but significant changes that are employed towards establishing the *approximate* date of the observed car, and we here attempt to identify some of these.

The Ford Motor Company made no great effort to establish the 1929 car as a different model that that of 1928, but the evolutionary changes were frequent and fairly well identified. On the other hand, the 1930 and 1931 models were considered by Ford to be quite different (and compared to the 1928-29 models, they *were*) but there is far less difference between the later two than one might suspect.

1928

A mark of the earliest cars is the open-ended bumper which was authorised for the first 200 only. The radiator is identical for 1928-29.

Shortly after production started, bumper ends were closed and strengthened as shown. Bumper bars are nickel-plated; bolt is painted.

These headlamp lenses with vertical flutes are typical of 1928.

The drum-shaped taillamp, typical of 1928, is made of brass, nickel-plated, and is stamped "Duo-Light".

1928 (and 1929) radiator caps and gasoline tank caps are brass castings, nickel-plated. This 1928 radiator cap has a higher crown than the gasoline cap (right), but in 1929, they were alike.

The gasoline tank cap has a very small hole at the center to prevent a vacuum lock as gasoline flows from bottom of the tank.

The early hoods were fitted with louvres the top edge of which paralleled the lower edge of the hood. This resulted in the curious, sloping, effect of the top line as shown here. The rear-most louvres are almost 5/8 inches shorter than those towards the front.

By mid-1928, the design had changed, and the louvres were redesigned for a more pleasing effect in which their top edge now paralleled the hinge line.

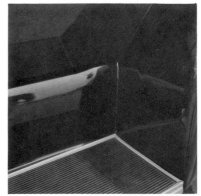

With the installation of the dual-brake system in June of 1928, a characteristic bulge appeared in the splash apron to allow clearance for the pull rods.

The splash apron is one continuous piece from the fender line back.

The running board is rubber-surfaced, with a characteristic of the 1928 & 1929 cover being this long vertical rib. A zinc trim, initially chrome plated, was used and later omitted and the zinc merely buffed.

The earliest center bumper clamp bears Ford script and "Made in USA". It was shortly replaced by a similar part with script only. After May of 1928, an oval part, similar to the outer clamps (right) but without the script was used.

Rear bumper clamps carried the Ford script until about March of 1928 after which they were plain.

The dashboard is a satin finished steel stamping. Speedometer has both odometer and also a resettable trip indicator. The notch, at the side of the speedometer mounting hole accomodates the reset knob.

The handbrake lever is a pistol-grip style, and is located at the left side of the compartment. This indicates an early single-brake system which was used until June of 1928, after which the hand brake lever was relocated directly in front of the gear shift lever.

The earliest ammeters had Ford script on face, being a carry-over from Model T. Quite soon, the script was deleted. Note early gearshift knob.

The words ON and OFF at the ignition switch, were dropped in November of 1928. By 1929, there was no lettering to aid driver.

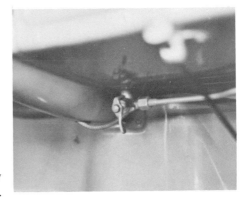

A fuel shut-off valve under the gas tank requires only a quarter turn to stop flow.

This front bumper center clamp is the earliest style, a direct carry-over from the Model T lines.

Shortly afterwards, this chrome-capped stamping was employed. This lasted to about June of 1928.

After June of 1928, and until the end of production, all Model A's employed this design (left). The part was a chrome plated stamping through 1929, and was changed to a stainless steel clad part in late 1930 (below).

A sheet-metal shroud was placed around the fan to aid cooling and was employed through 1928.

The early generator was a five-brush unit, rather squat, and known as the Powerhouse generator. At first furnished with a cut-out mounted to the side, as shown here, later versions had the cut-out on top of the generator.

The early, rectangular, starter switch is activated by an oddly shaped push rod on the very earliest of Model A. Only a relatively few had this feature.

The 1928-29 tube valve stem cover is this nickel-plated metal shroud. A flat nut, about 3/4 inch in diameter is installed first to hold stem rigid and to provide a locking surface for the cap.

The early 1928 AR type wheel was used until about June of that year when the separate emergency brake system was introduced. The tire size for all 1928-29 models is 4:50 x 21.

Ford script, accompanied by the words "Made in USA", were similar to Model T parts. However, by summer of 1928, the "Made in USA" had been dropped.

This hub cap appears from late 1928 through the 1929 models.

Since bodies were painted separately, the bolted-on fender allows for the appearance of body color in the "well" behind the wheel.

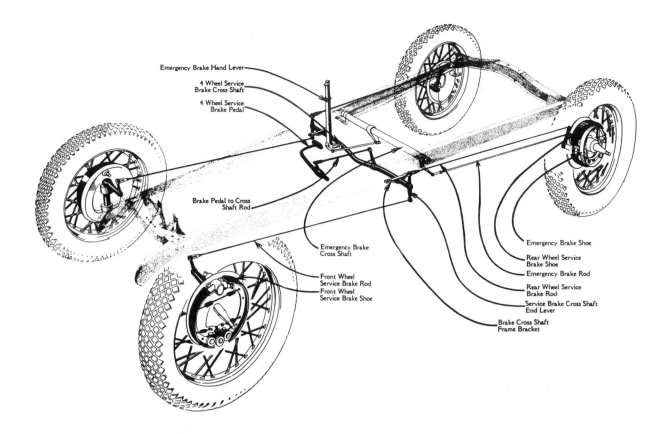

Emergency Brake Hand Lever
4 Wheel Service Brake Cross Shaft
4 Wheel Service Brake Pedal
Brake Pedal to Cross Shaft Rod
Emergency Brake Cross Shaft
Front Wheel Service Brake Rod
Front Wheel Service Brake Shoe

Emergency Brake Shoe
Rear Wheel Service Brake Shoe
Emergency Brake Rod
Rear Wheel Service Brake Rod
Service Brake Cross Shaft End Lever
Brake Cross Shaft Frame Bracket

Now lost in controvery is the basic *improvement* made in the braking system of the Ford cars with the introduction of the Model A. For the first time, brakes, of adequate surface, were installed on **all four wheels**. While previously, the two-rear-wheel brake system of the Model T had been accepted, the new Ford car now had a system of at least twice the numerical advantage.

An over-riding hand lever, mounted to the left of the driver, operated to the same effect as the foot pedal, and thus set all four wheel brakes. Since no separate emergency brake system was initially provided, the possible lock-up of the mechanical system raised controversy regarding the "unsafe" brake system. Almost immediately on introduction, it was seen that the car violated existing legislation in several states requiring separate emergency and service brake systems. (In theory, at least, even the Model T complied with these requirements by providing both the foot-operated transmission brake, and a separate hand-operated rear wheel "emergency" brake of doubtful value.

With bans on the new Ford proposed in Washington, D.C.. and in Pennsylvania, as openers, and with foreign countries such as Germany having issued legal restraints on its operation, the Ford car was hastily redesigned and a separate two-rear-wheel additional brake system installed requiring a change in the wheels and calling for the relocation of the handbrake lever to the center to operate on a cross-shaft the ends of which were fitted with levers mechanically connected to the two rear wheel brake levers.

This new "dual brake" system then persisted to the end of the Model A production with minor revision to the components. Among these were the substitution of a push-button handle for the squeeze grip in mid-1929 and another relocation of the hand brake to the right of the gear shift in the 1930 models.

late 1928-early 1929 (left)
late 1929 (center)
1930 & 1931 (right)

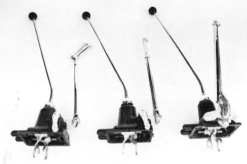

Model A control pedals were generally ribbed although some few early ones appear to have had smooth pedals. A foot rest is installed near the accelerator button.

A fuel shut-off is placed under the tank. In early 1928, this was changed to a stamping.

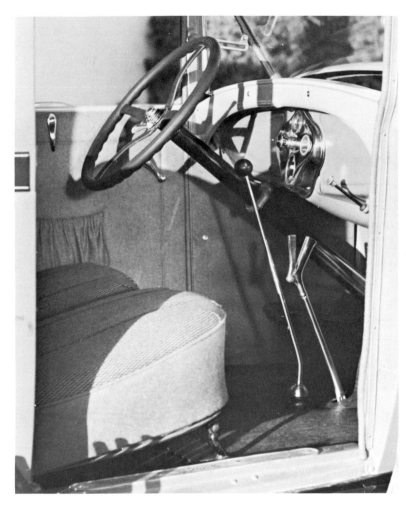

The pistol-grip hand brake lever was moved to a position directly in front of the gear shift lever in June of 1928.

This long-handled dip stick was used through 1928, and then replaced with one with a small circular handle.

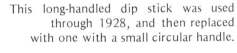

Lubrication fittings were added to the steering box about July of 1928. However, since the fittings allowed lighter weight lubricants to be added, they were replaced with pipe plugs less than a year later.

By late in 1929, the fan shroud behind the radiator (see page 35) had been deleted.

The Bendix starter, (on the right), was adopted for all production in September of 1928, and the lighter Abell unit discontinued.

By late 1928, several changes had been made in the engine compartment. Among these is a change in the shape of the starter switch and push rod (page 35).

The Powerhouse generator (left) was furnished well into 1928, but by the end of the year, it had been replaced by the conventional three-brush unit.

The familiar Ford script appears atop the generator cut-out.

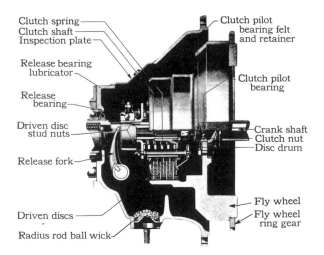

Clutch spring
Clutch shaft
Inspection plate
Release bearing lubricator
Release bearing
Driven disc stud nuts
Release fork
Driven discs
Radius rod ball wick

Clutch pilot bearing felt and retainer
Clutch pilot bearing
Crank shaft
Clutch nut
Disc drum
Fly wheel
Fly wheel ring gear

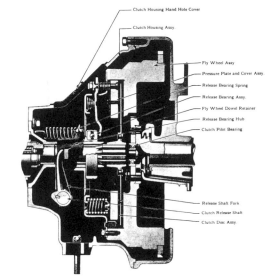

Clutch Housing Hand Hole Cover
Clutch Housing Assy.
Fly Wheel Assy.
Pressure Plate and Cover Assy.
Release Bearing Spring
Release Bearing Assy.
Fly Wheel Dowel Retainer
Release Bearing Hub
Clutch Pilot Bearing
Release Shaft Fork
Clutch Release Shaft
Clutch Disc Assy.

Over 500,000 Model A Fords were built using the dry multi-disc clutch similar to that of the Model T which worked in crankcase oil. Problems arose immediately with this dry version, and asbestos dust off of the driving discs packed into the hub splines to cause the clutch plates to hang up. In November of 1928, the multi-disc clutch was replaced with a new single-disc version, (right) which was so very acceptable that it was used, virtually unchanged, until 1948!

An obvious change in this typical late 1929 passenger compartment is the hand brake lever which is now of a push-button style rather than the earlier pistol grip. The lever is still located in front of the gear shift lever.

Early in 1929, these cowl lamps were made available through the Service Departments for those owners who may have wanted them. Cowl lights were installed as standard equipment on the Convertible Cabriolet and Town Sedans.

The two-light headlamp, bearing Ford script for the first time, introduced on the 1929 models had a distinctly different lens pattern than the earlier lamps.

Ford script also appears on lens itself.

Wheels were capped with Ford script. The "Made in USA" legend has been deleted.

This teacup-shaped tail light was introduced on the 1929 model. Stamped of brass, it was nickel-plated. Embossed on the top was DUOLAMP, not DUOLIGHT as on the 1928 light.

Early 1928 open models, as well as commercial types, were equipped with this hand-operated windshield wiper. This was a direct carry-over from the Model T line.

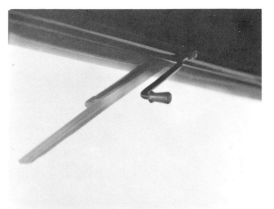

The six volt electric wiper motor was introduced early in 1928, and carried through well into 1930. An over-riding handle was provided as well as an On/Off control knob.

During the summer of 1929, the vacuum wiper was introduced. This was painted black to match the windshield frame.

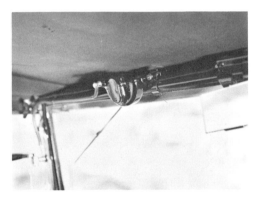

The chromed windshield wiper was installed on the chromed windshield frames of the roadsters and phaetons starting with the 1930 models.

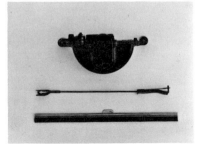

With a higher hood, smoother fairing, and a generally changed appearance, the 1930-31 cars appear to be quite different. than the earlier models. The radiator of the 1930 car has a painted insert at the bottom only, and the shell is stainless steel, buffed for appearance, but not plated. The core is made with oval tubes.

Late in 1930, the instrument panel was redesigned, and the former nickel-plated steel panel replaced with a "flatter" panel with a round speedometer. The new panel was made of chromed steel although a very few of the earliest ones were nickel-plated brass. Inserts at the top and bottom were painted, and the trip meter was dropped from the speedometer.

Cowl lights became more common and were installed on all deluxe models as well as on many standard models as accessories. Their arms were a bit shorter and more attractive than the 1929 style. Both cowl and also headlamps were made of stainless steel.

A stainless steel clad center bumper bolt was introduced during 1930, but for a large part of that year, the earlier chromed forging was used. Note the dumbell-shaped crank hole cover which replaced the teardrop shape during 1929.

A characteristic of the 1930 is this two-piece splash apron. In this design, the running board and adjacent portion of the splash apron are one piece and the forward section of the apron is welded to the fender. Thus it becomes necessary to raise the body to remove running board!. The pyramid design of matting is typical for 1930-31.

Fuel and radiator caps are now of two-piece construction with a stainless steel shell over a steel stamping, and are far less elaborate than the earlier style.

The trim around the running board is highly buffed zinc. Late in 1930, a stainless trim was introduced.

The car is now lowered by the use of 19" wheels. Tires are 4:75 x 19. Dealers began painting wheels, and by 1931, even the factory was doing so.

The 1930-31 valve stem cover is less attractive than the earlier style, but it permits tube to be inflated without removing the cap.

Originally of one-piece, stainless steel construction, 1930 hubcaps were quickly damaged, and shortly the factory changed their design to a stainless-steel *clad*, steel reinforced, two-piece design.

Although lacking documentation, the glass sediment bowl shown here appears to have become a production option late in 1929, and appears frequently.

Production ended on this earlier stoplight switch which had been mounted on the transmission with the introduction of a new design, frame mounted, which was connected so as to place its contact spring under compression except when foot brakes were applied.

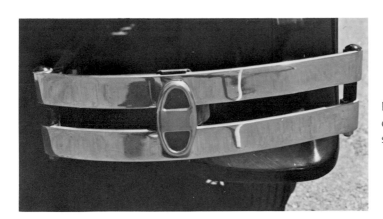

Rear bumper clamps continued into 1930 as chromed forgings, but late in this year became stainless steel clad stampings.

The tail lamp is now made of stainless steel. Unlike the red lens of 1929, this one, used in both 1930 and 1931, lights red for the marker function and amber for STOP.

In mid-'29, the squeeze-grip brake handle was replaced by a push-button grip. Then, starting with the 1930 models, the whole assembly was moved to a more convenient location to the right of the gear shift lever.

The radiator shell now has a painted insert at both top and also at the bottom. While the bottom insert is generally black, the upper one is painted body color. Frequently, however, both panels are painted body color as a matter of expediency.

The headlamps are not changed from 1930. A single bulb reflector is furnished when cowl lamps are installed.

An integral ON/OFF switch is furnished in a dashboard lamp installed behind the belt-rail above the instrument panel. The later 1931 panel had a more distinct trim surrounding the ribbed area.

Step plates are an accessory.

The running board now has a stainless steel trim on the outer edge only. A narrow border of flat rubber, about 3/8 inch wide, runs along the other three sides. The splash apron has returned to its earlier one-piece construction.

This fuel shut off was introduced on the engine side of the firewall in about April of 1931. Note the formed depression in the firewall.

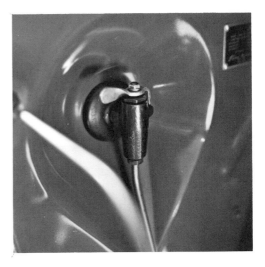

The sediment bulb, at this same time, was removed from the firewall and re-installed at the carburetor which has been modified for this purpose.

After March of 1931, the Ford script and its surrounding recessed oval were painted black.

The Phaetons
1928

The "Phaeton" was a new name for what had, until this year, been known as a "Touring" body style. With room for five passengers, this open-sided car was offered as a basic, unembellished, economy transportation car at $395, only $10 more than a Roadster, and only $15 more than the comparable Model T.

1928 Type 35-A Phaeton

Mr. Joe Crum, Oceanside, California

A very early car, this Phaeton displays the "open end" front bumper.

Rear view greatly resembles that of the previous year's Model T!

The single horn, and early headlamps, are suspended from a cross bar affixed to the fenders.

The radiator shell is nickel-plated steel. Headlamp lens has vertical flutes only. The oval emblem on the radiator shell has Ford script against a dark blue background. The crank hole cover pivots for use.

The upper line of the louvres follows the line of the frame on early hoods. As a result, the hinge line seems to "rise".

Side curtains, frequently missing in restorations, were factory-issue as part of the car. When installed, they did provide a fairly comfortable closed car effect.

Side curtains were made of a material similar to top. The "windows" were made of celluloid, a fairly inflexible material which frequently cracked when rolled.

The metal portions of the top socket assembly are painted black, not body color.

Note the absence of outside door handles. The flap in the side curtains, to allow driver to extend arm for signalling, is not original, but is considered a good safety idea.

The wooden seat frame is sheet-metal covered, and upholstered, offering a distinctive curve.

The body had been painted prior to assembly, hence, sides of body seen under rear fender displays body color.

The single stripe around the back becomes two as it moves forward from the lower edge of the top socket. A plug conceals the threaded socket into which top saddles are installed to support a lowered top.

Note the treatment of the stripe pattern in this area which is unique to the phaeton. The receptacle is employed when attaching side curtains.

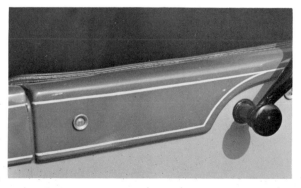

A compartment which extended all the way to the rear under the back seat was furnished for the storage of side curtains.

The seat cushions are upholstered with a seam sewn across the cushion at about one third the distance to the rear. The seat risers are made of sheet metal.

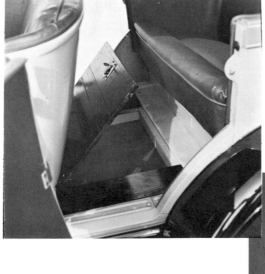

The side curtain compartment was reached by removing the rubber floor mat and lifting a hinged section in the wooden floorboards. A concealed latch offered a finger-pull handle.

One-piece splash aprons flow to metal, rubber-covered, running boards. Both sides of car use same running board, the trim of which is chrome-plated zinc. Note the early hood with its non-parallel hinge- and louvre top- lines.

The steering wheel is 17" in diameter. Made of red rubber, this very early wheel has no notches or grooves as are found on later ones. The light switch is nickel-plated, and frames the hard rubber horn button.

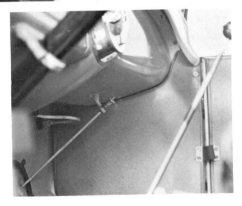

The combination choke and mixture-adjustment rod is quite short, and well-recessed. The shift lever is straight, and crowned by a hard rubber knob.

The steering wheel is essentially "flat".

The heart-shaped instrument cluster contains a fuel gage (upper), dashlight (center), ammeter (right), and oval speedometer (bottom) . The words ON and OFF appear on the escutcheon plate of the ignition lock.

The windshield brackets and frame are painted black. After December of 1927, these items were painted body color.

The windshield is hinged near the top, and can be opened out for additional ventilation. A locking nickel-plated thumbscrew is used to hold it in the open position.

A motor-driven horn is suspended under the left headlamp. Although horns were furnished by five independent manufacturers, they were essentially alike. This one is a Sparton, others included Ames, E.A., Stewart-Warner, and G.M.I.

Headlamp lenses have vertical lines only. The headlamp bulbs are dual-filament for "bright" and "dim".

The radiator and fuel tank caps were nickel-plated brass castings, similar but for the vent hole in the fuel tank cap. The Ford script is on a dark blue enamel escutcheon plate.

Closed end rear bumpers appear on this car, but the front bumper is the open ended type.

The early drum-shaped rear tail light is nickel-plated, and contains a dual filament bulb for stop and marker functions.

This spare wheel illustrates the correct installation, with the tube stem pointed down, and the hubcap script in horizontal position. This relationship was a matter of Ford policy on all wheels. The tire cover is an accessory, first available in January of 1928.

These early "AR" style wheels differ in design from the later type used with the separate emergency brake system starting in June of 1928.

The small hubcaps and 21" wheels are a characteristic of the 1928-29 style.

The design of the tread lead to the designation "diamond tread".

These *original* Goodyear tires have a unique diamond pattern on the sidewalls as shown here.

The wheel lugs were initially similar to the late Model T. A tapered section bearing against the wheel was larger in diameter than the shank.

The hub cap is nickel-plated, and carries, in addition to the Ford script, the words "made in USA".

The open end bumper was used on earliest Model A only. Although records authorised them for first 200 cars only, this car, number 797, had open end bumper on front, closed on rear.

The spring shackles, perches, were forgings. Four-wheel hydraulic shock absorbers were introduced on Ford line with Model A.

The internal-expanding brake linings could be adjusted by turning the hex stud at top of wheel which rotated a cam inside to spread brake shoes.

The Ford script on the rear bumper clamps appeared on early cars, but was deleted in June of 1928.

Another view which emphasises
the lines of the early hood.

The hood on this car is extremely early and illustrates the manner in which Ford operated to use up old parts. The handle on the right side is the new Model A design, but the one on the left side is definitely a Model T item!

A spring-loaded latching hook secures the hood.
Originally a forging, it became a stamping
during 1929.

A cast sediment bowl, with a forged handle, is affixed to the firewall under a patent data plate.

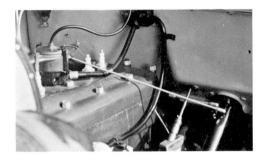

A connecting rod extends from the base of the steering column to rotate distributor for ADVANCE or RETARD of spark timing. A similar rod passes behind the engine to a bellcrank which is linked to the throttle plate in the carburetor.

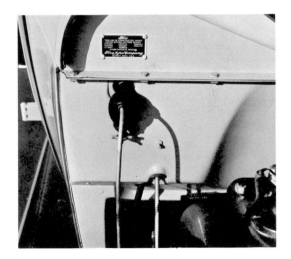

The choke-and-mixture adjustment rod extends through the firewall to the carburetor.
(see page 55 for view of upper end)

The ignition coil bears the Ford script, and is mounted on the wall of the fuel tank.

For better combustion, the fuel is preheated by having the intake manifold heated by the exhaust. The choke arm of this early Zenith single-venturi carburetor lacks the extension at the bottom which was added later to permit cranking from the front.

The red rubber distributor commutates the high voltage to the spark plugs, and also houses the breaker points in the primary circuit of the coil. These points are interrupted by a rotating cam driven from the camshaft. The correct spark plugs, not shown here, are Champion C-4.

A metal conduit runs from the terminal block, and houses the generator electrical wiring.

A two-bladed fan is used for cooling.
A sheet-metal shroud around blade
acts as a venturi tube.

The red rubber hose is secured by two steel
clamps to cast fittings bolted to the block.

This long-handled dip-stick was replaced with a
short, circular style in January of 1929.

The "square", early, starter switch is mounted
atop the starter. Pressing the starter button
on the floor, (above the accelerator button)
depressed the switch through the push rod.

This early Powerhouse generator has a strap-metal brace
(partly concealed behind fan belt). The rear cover
is aluminum, and is not painted.

The earliest of the Model A cars were equipped with a single four-wheel brake system. Depressing the foot pedal, *or* pulling back on the left-hand brake lever, would "set" all four brakes. In this system, two separate short cross-shafts (center photo) were employed with an equalizing linkage between them, and the two activating levers were keyed to it.

In December of 1927, non-adjustable brake rods were introduced, (and eliminated in November of that year). In this system, the adjustable clevis at the ends of the brake rods were abandoned for fixed eyes (lower picture).

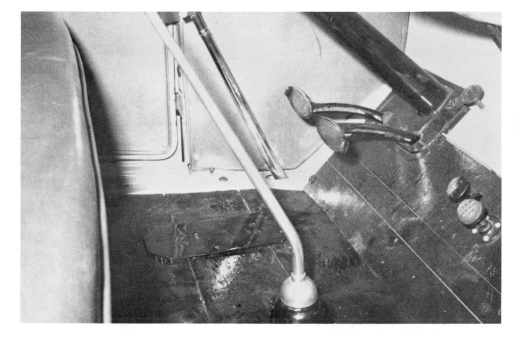

With rubber floor mat removed, the original floorboards of this car may be seen. The foot pedals have ribbed patterns, but some early cars had smooth pedals. The left-side brake handle indicates an original single-brake system.

1929 Type 35-A Phaeton   *Mr. Ragner Lindman, Anaheim, California*

Offered as a low-cost, economy vehicle, the Phaeton was manufactured with little in the way of dress-up items.

Starting with the 1929 models, outside door handles became standard. Kits were offered by the Dealers for the conversion of 1928 models.

The very necessary draft deflectors, (wind wings), *were* furnished as standard equipment on the 1929 models.

These adjustable windwing brackets were introduced late in 1929. By turning a thumbscrew between the arms, a change in spacing to accommodate different thicknesses of glass could be had.

This rubber-like button was furnished to plug the holes into which the top rests were inserted when the top was lowered. Although furnished with the car as standard equipment, the top rests were not installed at the factory.

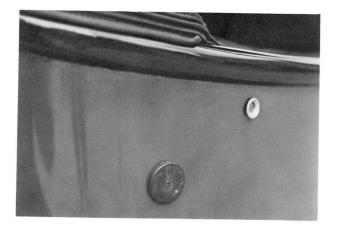

1929 Type 35-A Phaeton   *Mr. Harry Rinker, Costa Mesa, California*

Heavily laden with era accessories, the appearance of the basic car is markedly changed.

Windwings were added this year as standard equipment, (along with outside door handles), but the glass was generally plain, not etched. The snap fasteners are used when installing the side curtains.

Of the many accessories on this car, many are obvious in this view. These include: cowl lamps, right-hand welled fender, white wall tires, spare tire cover & mirror, spotlamp, step plates, and trunk, as well as the radiator stone guard & motometer.

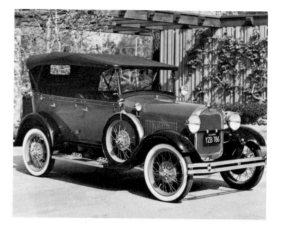

The rear-mounted trunk conforms to the curve of the body, and the right-hand tail lamp is considered a good safety accessory. The top saddles, inserted in this view, are ordinarily not installed, and their sockets plugged unless top is to be folded.

This car has accessory dual side mounts, mirrors, and cowl lamps, all of which add apparent width to the basic appearance of the unembellished car (below).

The stone guard and motometer are more common accessories than the cowl lamps and spotlight.

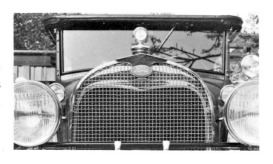

The right-hand welled fender and spare wheel is a most unusual option on the 1929 Phaeton. Although in 1929, welled fenders *could* have been furnished by the factory, six-wheel installations were indeed rare.

Cowl lamps were first introduced on Ford cars in January of 1929 on the Town Sedan and the Convertible Cabriolet, and became popular accessories for other models.

Welled front fenders were first made available as factory installations starting with the 1929 models although Dealers had been offering these fenders as early as late 1928.

The accessory trunk conceals a further accessory, the trunk rack which supports it. Note the cup-shaped taillight, characteristic of 1929.

The top sockets are steel, cross bows are wood. The metal parts are painted black, and cross bows cloth-wrapped.

The leather straps around the accessory trunk add to the general appearance. Right hand taillight is an accessory.

1930 Type 35A Phaeton   *Mr. Joel Feldman, Los Angeles, California*

The standard Phaeton had no cowl lights.

The windshield frame is painted, not plated.

Only one tail lamp, on the left rear, is furnished.

The rear window frame is painted a flat black, not chromed. The spare tire is mounted at the rear.

Side curtains are standard issue with this open car. When installed, the interior is reasonably weathertight. The curtains fasten to snap fasteners near the top edge of the doors (right). Their top edge bears against a short flap inserted under the edge of the top.

The rearmost of the side curtains fasten to the top and are installed *inside* the top socket.

Side curtains are supported by steel rods inserted into holes in the door sill. The bulge caused by one such curtain rod shows clearly.

The windwing brackets must be loosened and the glass turned in in order to install side curtains. Those fasteners affixed to the side of the car are female snap type while those on the windshield posts are male and fit sockets in the curtains.

Wheels are 19" diameter, lowering car a full
inch from last year's model. Whitewall tires
are an accessory.

The hood louvres are set into an
embossed rectangular section
to add strength.

With the doors all hinged at the front, an easy, simultaneous entry to both the front and the
rear seats may be made. The doors are two inches wider than the 1928-29 body style, and the
pillar is consequently narrower than last year.

A metal-covered wooden framework forms the seat back and extends
from one pillar to the other to provide support for the rear door.
The front door is suspended from the cowl section.

This horn is a Sparton although others look quite similar.

The rear door hinges protrude abruptly from the body.

This two-piece splash apron is a distinctive mark of the 1930 models.

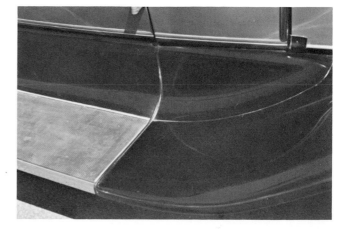

The windwings are standard, and are bolted
into the windshield stanchions.

The newly-designed windshield stanchions are pressed
from stainless steel. With the top lowered, the
windwings could be folded back against the
glass and the entire windshield rotated to
fold flat against the cowl.

The lower section of the windshield frame is
faired smartly into the cowl, and painted
for best effect.

1928 Type 35-A Phaeton   *Mr. Joseph Crum, Oceanside, California*

1929 Type 35-A Phaeton   *Mr. Ragner Lindman, Anaheim, California*

1931 Type 35-B Phaeton   *Mr Fred Meyers, Escondido, California*

1930 Type 35-B Phaeton   *Mr. Joel Feldman, Los Angeles, California*

1930 Type 180-A Phaeton　　　　　*Mr. Howard Lambke, Orange, California*

1931 Type 400-A Convertible Sedan　　*Mr. David Treichell, South Gate, California*

1929 Type 40-A Roadster   *Mr Jack Hilton, Long Beach, California*

1931 Type 40-B Deluxe Roadster   *Mr. Herbert Haynes, Jr., Phoenix, Arizona*

1930 Type 68-B Convertible Cabriolet   *Mr. Jack Tyrrell, Reno, Nevada*

1931 Type 68-C Convertible Cabriolet   *Mr. Ted Dobbins, South Gate, California*

1930 Type 45-B standard Coupe   *Mr. Edgar Orange, Los Angeles, California*

1931 Type 45-B Deluxe Coupe   *Dr. William Ingwersen, South Gate, California*

1928 Type 54-A Business Coupe   *Mr. Fred Meyers, Escondido, California*

1929 Type 50-A Sport Coupe   *Mr. Charles Davies, Long Beach, California*

The rearview mirror bracket clamps to the windshield frame.

An electric windshield wiper, painted black, is installed in this car.

Loosening the upper thumbscrew enables the bottom of the windshield to be rotated outward. For still more ventilation, the entire windshield assembly may be rotated into a horizontal position against the cowl by releasing the top fasteners and loosening the lower thumbscrews.

The trim for the 1930 standard Phaeton is essentially all-black.
The top is made of a long-short grained artificial leather,
and the sockets are painted black.

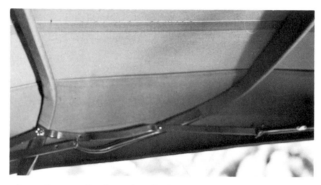

A pad runs the length of the top on either side
to provide a more rounded shape.

The rear curtain window frame is painted black.

The seats, of artificial leather, are pleated.

Both front and rear seats have eleven pleats.

Cardboard panels, covered with a material resembling that of the seats, are installed at the doors, pillars, and kick panels. Note the distinctive pattern of the stitching.

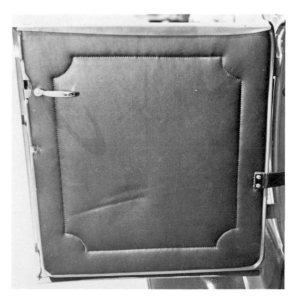

This glass bowl fuel filter became available early in 1930 in place of the earlier cast style although both continued to be used.

The 1930 hood folds back on itself, allowing an easy access to the engine compartment.

This rubber bumper is installed on the sill to provide a firm back-up for the hood when latched.

1930 Type 180-A Deluxe Phaeton   *Mr. Howard Lambke, Orange, California*

One large door on each side, in place of the two
of the standard Phaeton, give the car
a rakish look.

Furnished as a five-wheel car, this right-hand fender-
mounted sixth wheel is a fashionable accessory.

The windshield frame and stanchions are chrome plated as are the windwing brackets.

Two individual front seats are racy in appearance.

The bench-type rear seat is entered by folding the front seat (below left) to gain access.

An unusual storage pocket for the side curtains is placed behind the rear seat.

The upper edge of the body is depressed slightly at the rear to allow the top to fold into a nearly horizontal position. The long rear top socket contains a hole in its lower end into which fits a pin in the top assembly when folded, this to give rigidity.

The top saddles are chrome-plated brass castings, threaded to screw into receptacle in body.

This unusual inside door handle operates from a position well forward on the door.

The accessory metal tire cover has a painted faceplate and a chromed outer ring.

1931 Type 35-A standard Phaeton   *Mr. Fred Meyers, Escondido, California*

The Phaeton, a low-priced economy model, ordinarily had a rear mounted spare tire, but this car has received accessory welled fenders and side-mounted spare tires as well as cowl lights to dress it up. Although authentic accessories, neither would have appeared in the original except by special order.

The top is of a black rubber-like material with a distinct grain. The sockets are painted black.

A thumb-screw locks the top frame assembly in the extended position.

The windshield frame on this standard Phaeton is painted black.

The folding portion of the windshield stanchion is polished stainless steel.

The insert at the top of the radiator shell is painted body color.

The Ford script insert in the upper radiator shell is painted black on cars produced after about March of that year.

The painted insert at the lower end of the radiator shell is generally painted black although many were painted to match upper panel. The dumb-bell shaped crank hole cover has been in use since 1929.

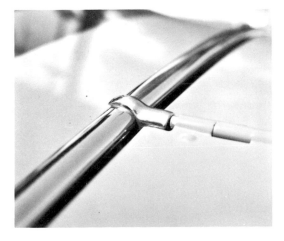

The right-hand tail light is an accessory. By late in 1931, Dealers were being urged by the factory to recommend this installation.

This is the "later" style hood cleat introduced with 1930 models, and having only two mounting screws at the base. Compare with earlier style on page 195.

This deluxe accessory dress-up clip secures the rear edge of the hood hinge pin.

The running board matting now has a self-edge border on three sides. A stainless steel moulding is placed at the outer edge only.

The splash apron has again become one-piece and the running board is a separate assembly.

Top saddles, which support the lowered top, were furnished as accessory parts. When the top was to be folded, they were screwed into holes which were otherwise plugged.

1928 Model A Phaeton

1931 Model A Phaeton

Like the Phaeton, the Roadster was offered as a low-priced basic transportation car. It was priced at only $385, with an optional extra cost rumble seat, only $35 more than the similar Model T. The 1928 models, in similar fashion to the Phaetons, did not have outside door handles or windwings, but were otherwise essentially identical to the 1929 model pictured here.

1929 Type 40-A Roadster   *Mr. Jack Hilton, Long Beach, California*

These windwings became standard on the 1929 models and were then offered as an accessory for the earlier cars by the Dealers.

Outside door handles were added to the 1929 models and kits were then made available by the Dealers for the earlier cars.

The newly added wind wings serve to defect the passing air around the front seat passengers.

The loop on the top assembly just above the windshield serves as an anchor point for a leather strap which was passed through it and around the folded top to prevent chafing the loose canvas.

This nickeled rail provides both for passenger convenience, and also serves to protect the rear deck from the folded top assembly.

The brown artificial leather of the rumble seat is not pleated.

The rumble seat compartment is lined with a brown cardboard grained to resemble that of the seats themselves.

This latch secured the hooked tongue of the rumble seat latch. Note its location, and compare with that on page 166.

A locking T handle is provided to secure the rumble seat.

A clip appears at the rear of the radiator to hold the forward edge of the hood in the open position.

This inside door handle was provided starting with the introduction of outside door handles in the 1929 model.

The top assembly is made of steel and painted black. The prop nut is also black.

Two square access step plates were provided with rumble seats. This one on the right rear fender is accompanied by another affixed to the rear bumper bracket.

1929 Type 40-A Roadster

Mr. Richard Palmer, Encino, California

This is an unusual right-hand drive, New Zealand-sold car. Its engine number, CA 91051, indicates that it was built in Canada, as was the custom, and then assembled in New Zealand. First sold on July 7, 1929, the car's service record was meticulously documented as the car passed through the hands of three previous owners and found its way to Hawaii where it was purchased by the present owner in 1971. Little, if any, restoration work has been done on the car, and it thus appears in these pages as an example of a most unique Model A.

Although at first glance it might appear that this picture has been printed backwards because of the position of the steering wheel, a glance at the license plate assures that this is an unusual, right-hand drive, car.

With right-hand drive, the taillamp is placed on the right rear fender, the step plates to the rumble seat on the left.

A leatherette top boot protects the folded top.
This accessory was first offered in January of 1928.

The rumble seat latching handle is shown in the "open" position. With handle turned to face the rear of the car, the cover is latched tight. A square access plate is installed on the left rear fender.

The spare tire cover is an accessory first offered in the USA in January of 1928.

Missing, and more obvious in this view, is the hand-operated windshield wiper.

The drum-shaped rear lamp is the same as domestic lamps, but the forged bracket which holds it is the mirror-image of the USA types. The difference is caused by the need to suspend the lamp from the right side of the car.

Entry to the driver's seat is from the right.

The steering wheel is red rubber, and the controls are similar to domestic models with the spark on the left and the throttle on the right.

The clock, mounted on the steering column, is an accessory.

The squeeze-grip hand brake is located just ahead of the gear shift lever. The foot accelerator, on the right, is provided with a foot rest.

"Foreign" cars, including English- and Canadian-built vehicles, were equipped with round, rather than oblong, pedals as are found on domestic models.

There is no change in the position of the instruments or panel. The keylock switch on this car is a replacement.

The choke rod, extending under the fuel tank in the normal manner, is found to be conveniently placed for use by the right-hand drive operator.

Although manufactured in mid-1929, this "foreign" car still uses the headlight and lens typical of the 1928 domestic production.

The nickel-plated radiator shell is embellished by an accessory quail.

The chrome-plated bumpers have closed ends.

Mounting of the early drum taillamp to the right rear fender calls for a special forged bracket unlike those on domestic cars.

Adding the separate emergency brake system in early 1928 necessitated this bulge in the splash aprons to clear the secondary brake rods.

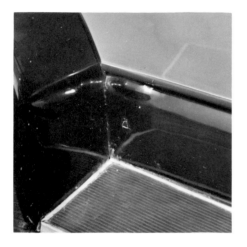

The top boot is an accessory which greatly adds to the appearance.

The hood louvres parallel the hinge line.

The Powerhouse generator is an early item which had disappeared from domestic production long before the July 1929 manufacturing date of this New Zealand car.

The Model A engine was originally rigidly mounted in four places, but the effect of engine vibration was shortly reduced when in November of 1928, a new, three point, spring suspension was introduced on domestic models. This change, however, had not yet reached this "foreign" car manufactured in 1929.

In this view, the distributor cap has been removed to permit a view of the breaker points.

carburetor is not original

The right-hand drive is eagerly sought by U.S. collectors due to its novelty here. These views illustrate the mechanisms employed to convert the lower end motions of the hand-operated spark and throttle levers into usable motions at the distributor and carburetor. Attention is directed to the intake manifold which provides a pivot for the spark linkage.

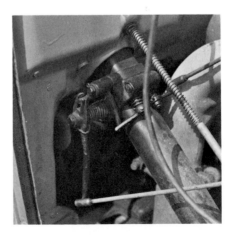

An early 1929 car, this Roadster has the headlamps
and the drum taillamp more typical of the 1928
style. Fitted with an accessory folding windshield, the entire appearance of the car is
changed from the more typical 1929 (pg 102).

1929 Type 40-A Roadster   *Mr. Ernie Ball, Costa Mesa, California*

The welled front fenders were not standard, but *were*
available as an optional extra cost equipment item
after January of 1929. While possibly serving to
dress up the car, it is not truly representative
of the original manufacturing configuration.

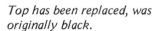

Top has been replaced, was originally black.

With the introduction of outside door handles on the 1929 models, these inside handles were also installed in place of the earlier style which protruded through top edge of the door.

This very desirable accessory folding windshield stanchion permits the windshield to be folded flat on the cowl.

Shown for comparison is a standard 1929 windshield lower section. Note similarity to the accessory frame in that area.

The 1930 Roadster was a distinct departure from the 1928-29 style. Featuring a folding windshield which could be laid flat against the cowl, and with a smoothly faired cowl section, higher sides, and wider doors, the racy appearance was further enhanced by the flow of the moulding trim which started at the radiator, and ran down the sides to the rear of the car.

Initially offered as a single, standard, model, without cowl lamps or side mounts, it was enhanced by both of these items plus a new, lower, top and windshield, and re-introduced as an additional new model, the Deluxe Roadster, in August of 1930.

Shown here are a 1930 Deluxe Roadster (on the right) and a 1930 standard Roadster which has been fitted with accessory cowl lamps and side mounts. While the Deluxe Roadster did have a tan top, the original standard Roadster top was black.

The 1930 Deluxe Roadster featured a left-front fender-mounted spare wheel and tire, and a rear-mounted luggage rack. The tire cover itself is an accessory.

The side curtains were furnished as standard equipment with the car although rumble seat passengers had little protection from the weather.

Full-width rear bumpers were introduced on the 1930 Deluxe Roadster. The standard Roadster continued to use the two individual rear fender guards.

The standard Roadster retained the painted top assembly with a somewhat different profile, and had a higher windshield and stanchion than the Deluxe Roadster. The wind-wing mirror is an accessory.

The Deluxe Roadster featured a chromed top assembly which displays a portion of its varnished rear bow. The windshield stanchion is only 13" high, one inch shorter than the standard models, and the windshield itself is thus one inch lower. The outside mirror was standard on the Deluxe models which had no inside rear-view mirror.

Windwings were included as standard equipment on both Roadsters.

Virtually the only difference between *these* 1931 Deluxe Roadsters and the 1930 models appears from this view to be limited to the radiator shell. The side-mounted spare wheel, however, is as accessory.

Suggesting that Ford may have been less careful than today's restorers, the pleats on this original 1931 Deluxe Roadster do not line up where seat and back cushion join. The Deluxe Roadster had thirteen pleats as shown here, standard Roadster had only seven.

Starting with the 1931 models, wheels were painted at the factory to match the color of the stripe, (earlier, many were done by the Dealers on request). The tire cover is an accessory.

1931 Type 40-B standard Roadster　　　　Mr. Dennis Lutz, Fallbrook, California

The standard Roadster was still considered to be the basic low-cost Ford, and was offered with artificial leather upholstery of a quality just below that used in the Deluxe. Other than a lower windshield and top, cowl lamps, and some more elaborate trim items on the Deluxe, there really was little difference between the two models.

The spare tire was mounted on the rear on standard Roadsters which were equipped with cowl lamps only on special order. Note the continued use of the two piece fender guards rather than the full-width cross-bar bumper as used on the 1930 Deluxe Roadster (right).

The 1931 Deluxe Roadster returned to an earlier style and was produced with the rear-mounted spare tire rather than a fender mount. This very original car illustrates this condition as well as the lack of a right-hand tail lamp which would have interfered with access to the rumble seat.

1931 Type 40-B Deluxe Roadster *Mr. Jay Guion, Avalon, California*

The sporty appearance of the Deluxe Roadster is hightened by simple lines.

An optional rumble seat offered room for passengers or for storage, and an accessory tire cover dresses up the view from the rear.

1931

The fender-mounted spare tire, (and the rear-mounted luggage rack), were extra cost, accessories in 1931.
Unless so ordered, the Deluxe Roadster was furnished with the spare at the rear.

1931 Type 40-B Deluxe Roadster   *Mr. Herbert Haynes, Jr., Phoenix, Arizona*

The top is of tan fabric installed over a chromed steel and wood frame. Snap fasteners at the lower rear permit the complete removal of the entire assembly.

The smoothly faired cowl section is typical of 1930-31, but the one-piece splash apron quickly identifies this as a '31.

Two chromed rails offer a hand-hold for rumble seat passengers and also act as a rest for the top when folded back.

While the upper radiator panel is painted body color, the lower panel is generally painted black.

The stripe begins at the radiator and travels all the way to the rear.

Beginning in 1931, the wheels were painted at the factory to match the color of the stripe.

Only the upper section of the folding windshield stanchion was chromed. The lower section continues to be painted. A hole, apparently for an accessory rear-view mirror, has been drilled into this stanchion.

Cowl lamps were furnished as standard equipment on the Deluxe Roadsters, and were available as accessories for use on the standard Roadster.

The pleated seats of the Deluxe Roadster were done in brown leather. Although also pleated, the standard Roadster was upholstered in black artificial leather.

Through early 1931, the fuel tank shut-off remained under the gas tank.

The Convertible Cabriolet was introduced in early 1928, although production did not roll until March or April. This luxury model offered the advantages of both a closed car and a Roadster, and soon reached a fairly high popularity. The model continued to the end of Model A production.

1929 Type 68-A Convertible Cabriolet
Mr. Carroll Vaughn Jr., North Hollywood, California

Peculiar to the Convertible Cabriolet is the paint scheme of the rear deck which is all brown. The whitewall tires and locking band on the rear-mounted spare tire are accessories although the position of the tire, at the rear, is standard for the car.

With the top lowered, and the rumble seat open, the Convertible Cabriolet offers much of the sporty appearance of a Roadster.

Cowl lamps, gone since the mid-twenties, returned to the Fords in January of 1929 with the introduction of the Convertible Cabriolet and the Town Sedan.

The rumble seat passengers were given a bit of wind protection by the bulk of the folded top which does not lie quite so flat as it does on the Roadster.

The coupe pillar found on most other 1929 models is eliminated in this smoothly-faired front cowl section. The roll-down windows are chrome plated, but the windshield and the wiper motor are painted.

Chromed folding landau irons are secured with oversized prop nuts.

This bracket serves to stiffen the window frame when the top is raised.

A good bit of the bulk of the folded top is due to the window frame which folds with it.

The rumble seat is plain, not pleated, and is done in artificial leather. The interior, however, received a far more extravagant cloth trim.

1930 Type 68-B Convertible Cabriolet   *Mr. Jack Tyrrell, Reno, Nevada*

The welled front fender, rear luggage rack, and white side wall tires are accessories.

The entire rear deck section of the Convertible Cabriolet is painted upper body color including the rumble seat lid.

The chromed cowl band and the cowl lamps are standard for the Convertible Cabriolet, the tire cover is an accessory as is the rear view mirror.

Originally, the Convertible Cabriolet had a rear-mounted spare tire, but many owners preferred the sporty appearance of the side mount.

When windows are lowered, there is no frame left exposed around the door.

In this view, the resemblence to the Roadster is most striking.

The wiper motor is painted black although the windshield is plated. After June of 1930, the electric wiper was replaced with a chromed vacuum operated unit.

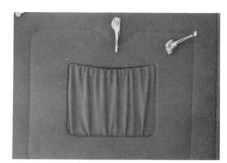

A door pocket is provided in each front door.

The seats are upholstered in tan bedford cord. Until February of 1930, a grey checked cloth interior was furnished as a carry-over from the 1929 interior.

The door panels are trimmed nicely in bedford cord. After July, this was changed to a broadcloth. At about that same time, a new, adjustable, front seat assembly was provided.

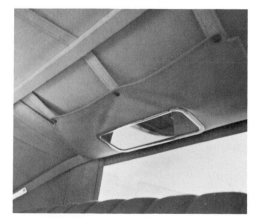

The rear window curtain can be folded upwards and suspended as shown. Starting in March, zippers were provided to hold the lowered flap in place.

This rear quarter treatment, with its folding landau irons, gave passengers a closed car feeling quite unlike that of the Roadster.

A round step plate, unlike the earlier 1928-'29 square step plate, on the right rear fender permits access to the rumble seat.

Seven wide pleats were provided on the rumble seat of the 1930 Convertible Cabriolet (in 1931 this was increased to 11).

The lower body color converges to a narrow wedge between the black fender and the dark upper body color applied across the entire back. (Trunk rack is an accessory)

1930 Type 68-B Convertible Cabriolet   *Mr. Ernie Harker, Whittier, California*

With the top folded, and especially when the windows are rolled down, only the appearance of the windshield quickly establishes that this is *not* the very similar Roadster. The spare tire cover, quail, and windwing mirror are accessories.

1930 Type 68-B Convertible Cabriolet

1931 Type 68-C Convertible Cabriolet

1931 Type 68-C Convertible Cabriolet   *Mr. Ted Dobbins, South Gate, California*

The "slant windshield" Convertible Cabriolet was introduced in the Spring of 1931 in a modernizing attempt by Ford. Deliveries did not actually begin until almost Summer.

The slope of the windshield is obvious in this view

The entire back of the car is painted upper body color.

The Convertible Cabriolet does not have the chromed top rests on the rear deck as found on Roadsters.

By 1931, Dealers were being urged by the factory to install right-hand rear tail lights, but installing them on rumble seat models blocked access.

The rear curtain window frames were made both of chrome plated steel and also from stainless steel.

The rear-mounted spare tires were not provided with a cover by the factory. These were considered to be "dress-up" items, and were available at extra cost only.

Cowl lamps were furnished with
the Convertible Cabriolet.

The side window frames (and the
windshield) are chromed.

The wiper motor is now mounted inside the
car (compare view on page 128). The rear
view mirror is a safety accessory.

Running along the forward edge of the top
is a groove which serves as a window slide.

The back of the window frame is hinged
at its lower edge to pivot back when
top is lowered.

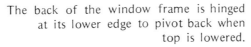

The folding landau irons on the slant windshield Convertible Cabriolet are slightly longer than the earlier style (pg 132) and have an offset at their lower end.

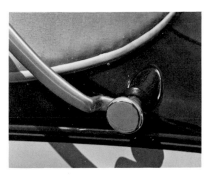

The dog-legged lower end of the '31 landau iron is fastened to a pivot on the body, unlike the earlier style which was secured to a point at the lower edge of the top.

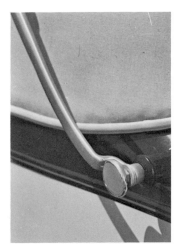

An accessory step plate emphasises the 1931 one-piece splash apron.

The wheels of the 1931 Convertible Cabriolet were painted black at the factory, but could have been repainted later.

Two zippers and three snap fasteners provide a smooth, snug, fit of the back curtain.

The rear window frame of this car is stainless steel, earlier, others were chromed.

This key-locked handle secures the rumble seat,

A round step-plate on the rear fender aids entry to the rumble seat.

The brown artificial leather upholstery with its eleven pleats looks most inviting.

The unlined top permits a view
of the supporting frame.

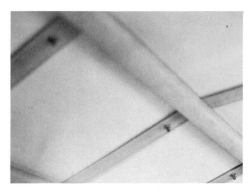

Snaps are attached to the webbing to
support the raised rear curtain.

Pockets were provided on both
front doors

The dashboard is striped to highlight the
embossed pattern in the metal. Generally
the pattern has rounded corners though.

The belt moulding and the garnish strips
around the top of the doors are
mahogany grained.

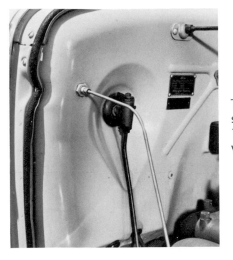

This recessed firewall, introduced on the slant windshield models in May of 1931, permitted the fuel shut-off valve to be relocated as shown.

Additional embossed stringers reinforce the new firewall.

The upper radiator panel is painted body color.

1928 Type 54-A Business Coupe   *Mr. Fred Meyers, Escondido, California*

Introduced in May of 1928, five months after the Model A first appeared, and just before the change from the single brake system in June of that year, this car is unusual since it does still employ its original single brake system.

The Business Coupe was produced with a trunk only. The rear-mounted spare wheel obscures a handle at the bottom of the panel.

Although greatly resembling the Convertible Cabriolet, the Business Coupe differs in that it retains the abrupt coupe pillar just ahead of the door.

The hood of this early model shows the apparent "drop" of the top line of the louvres which does not parallel the hinge line.

Unique to the Business Coupe and the similar Sport Coupe is the non-folding "soft" top and the door frame which surrounds the window glass. The windwings are accessories.

The top and visor are covered with a black artificial leather.

A black-painted electric windshield wiper is located under the visor.

The top material runs to the deck, and is pulled tight to eliminate the appearance of the bows. Although landau irons were not furnished as standard equipment, dress-up kits were made available by the Dealers.

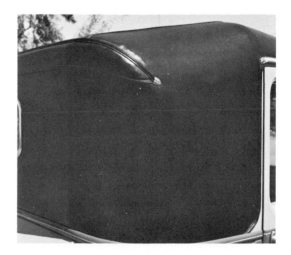

A lockable outside door handle is provided on the righthand door only.

The artificial leather top is stretched tightly over wooden bows.

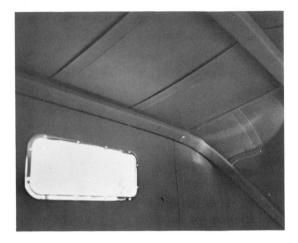

The windshield is painted lower body color as is upper door frame behind accessory windwings.

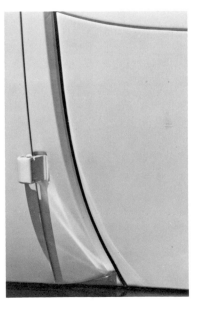

The sharply defined lower portion of the distinct coupe pillar.

Unlike the still earlier steering wheel on page 55, this red rubber wheel now has the familiar pattern of concentric grooves.

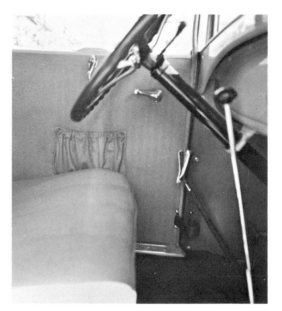

The lefthand brake indicates an early single-brake system. Note the inside door latch handles which differ from those used in open cars.

Some early models were furnished with this "mushroom" shaped gear shift knob in place of the more familiar ball. Note the script on ammeter and lettering above switch.

The spare wheel is correctly installed with its valve stem pointed downwards. The tire cover and lock are accessories. The window frame is nickel-plated.

The raised trunk lid exposes a large storage area. No interior trim was provided.

The moulding runs cleanly down to the lower back.

Although the rear tire appears to be in the way, there *is* adequate trunk access.

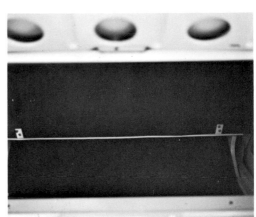

A cardboard seat back divides trunk from passenger compartment.

The basic design of the rear trunk section would permit a fairly easy conversion to a rumble seat since the platform and the hinge brackets are already installed.

A rotating tongue latches the deck lid and is concealed in its edge. A handle on the lid operates the latch.

1929 Type 54-A Business Coupe   Mr. Delbert Pantel, Chico, California

The "Porthole", used on the 1929 Business Coupe is unusual indeed. Introduced late in 1928, this too was considered an economy style and was offered for those whose business required inexpensive, basic, transportation. This was the only year in which the portholes were used, and they were then dropped until revived 27 years later on the 1956 Thunderbird.

The Business Coupe was manufactured with trunk only.

Top has been replaced, was originally black.

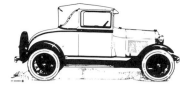

The (original) black artificial leather top material was continued forward and used to cover visor.

A larger rear window (pg 146), typical of the 1929 model, frames the oval porthole beyond. Until about May, the rear window frame was nickel-plated, after that it was painted.

This oval porthole window frame is nickel-plated to match rear window, others are painted.

The wheels were sometimes re-painted by the Dealers but were originally painted black by the factory. The step plates are an accessory, as is tire cover.

1928 Type 50-A Sport Coupe   *Mr. Charles Davies, Long Beach, California*

One of the six original Model A body styles, the Sport Coupe featured an appearance similar to that of the sporty Roadster, but afforded passengers the protection of a closed car. With roll-down windows and an attractive non-folding canvas top, the style leaped to an immediate popularity.

Fancier than the somewhat later Business Coupe which greatly resembles it, the difference is largely in the trim. The non-folding landau irons even became a popular accessory for Business Coupe owners who wanted just a bit more dash.

The rumble seat was a standard feature of the Sport Coupe, and the top was upholstered in a smart tan whipcord which also was used to cover the visor.

With rumble seat open or closed, the view from this angle is attractive.

Although the accessory spare tire cover was made to match top, the original was black.

The visor is covered with the same tan whipcord fabric as is used to cover top.

A door pull is formed into the window trim moulding.

The glass window rises in a fully framed door.

The bulge at the rear of these splash aprons would suggest that the car was built after June of 1928. Actually, this two-owner car was built on December 26, 1928.

The windshield is painted body color as is the supporting pillar.

The landau irons are non-folding and decorative only. The knobs and center section are nickel-plated, but the arms are painted body color.

The large rear window is held in a nickel-plated cast aluminum frame.

A number of well-placed padding materials give this top a softer and less awkward appearance than that of a Roadster or Convertible Cabriolet both of whose tops are designed for folding.

The Sport Coupe, from this angle, is difficult quickly to distinguish from the Convertible Cabriolet. A glance at the door framing the window glass helps to identify the car.

Manufactured very late in 1928, this car still was equipped with the drum taillamp.

The tan whipcord top is trimmed with brown artificial leather.

A locking T-shaped handle is provided for the rumble seat.

The 1928 rumble seat had no pleats. The upholstery is brown artificial leather.

Cardboard interior trim panels are used in the rumble seat and a rubber floor mat provided.

Door pockets are provided in the cloth-covered cardboard front door trim.

The Sport Coupe top is lined giving it more body. Snaps are installed in the webbing just behind the center bow to hold the rear window flap when it is raised.

The stamped date of 12 16 18 appears at the lower left corner of the fuel tank and is taken to be the assembly date of the car. Such date stamping was continued through late 1929.

Since the bodies were painted prior to assembly, the wells behind the bolted-on fenders show body color.

1929 Type 50-B Sport Coupe

Mr. Daniel Gale, Claremont, California

Largely identical with the 1928 model, an essential difference was the new choice of colors available for the top. These were: Tan whipcord, Dark Brown leather, Light Brown leather, or two-tone leather.

This particular car is also notable for its accessory dual spare tire carrier.

This accessory two-tire carrier is an unusual item. The tires, in turn, are protected by two accessory tire covers and an accessory center bumper bar.

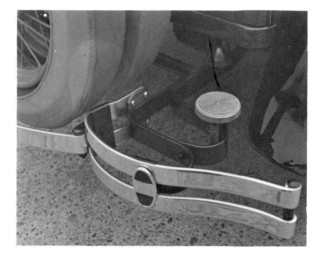

A rubber-covered step plate is mounted to the bumper bracket. A second step pad is affixed to the top of the right rear fender.

The rumble seat is standard in the Sport Coupe and provides additional seating for two passengers.

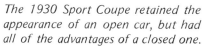

The 1930 Sport Coupe retained the appearance of an open car, but had all of the advantages of a closed one.

1930 Type 50-B Sport Coupe   *Mr. Jack Roggenbuck, Orange, California*

Shown for comparison is the 1928 Sport Coupe

The windwings and cowl lights on this car are accessories; they were not factory-installed.

With the rumble seat open, the car presents a truly sporty appearance. The rumble is standard on Sport Coupes, but the cowl lights and windwings are accessories as is the step plate and motometer.

The landau irons are non-folding and are furnished as standard equipment. The arms are painted body color.

This knob under the front seat permitted an adjustment of up to 3". Later, in July of 1931, this was changed to a rachet-type adjustment of about the same limits.

Other than the "typical" changes such as the splash aprons and radiator shell, there is little difference between the 1930 & 1931 Sport Coupes.

The Special Coupe is a distinctive style, produced for only about a year from July of 1928 to about mid-summer of the following year. Greatly resembling the steel-backed Coupe (which was discontinued for the manufacturing period of the Special Coupe), it differed in its use of a leather trim on the rear part of the passenger compartment.

1929 Type 49-A Special Coupe   *Mr. Eugene Show, San Diego, California*

The very distinctive appearance of the "leather back" Special Coupe is most striking from this angle.

The leather backing covers the rear section entirely.
Under it is a wire screen-and-wood framework.

No frame is furnished for the rear window. The
pull-down rear window shade is original.

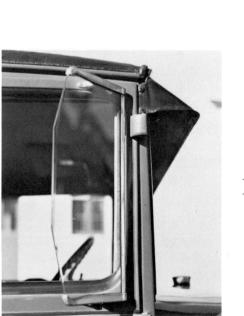

The leather-like top material also covers the visor.
The windwings are accessories.

The leather at the rear follows the body lines
in back of the quarter windows.

The spare tire is protected by an accessory cover, locking band, and lock.

A distinct seam is found where panels of leather are brought together. The metal body under it runs from about this point forward. Between the seams, the leather is merely stretched over wire screen and wooden slats.

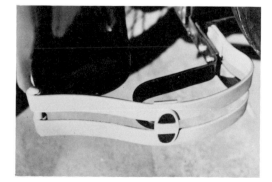

The Special Coupe was furnished with a trunk, not a rumble seat.
However, many of the items necessary to convert the trunk
to a rumble seat were already in place including the hinge
brackets and the seat platform.

*Production of this unique model, which began in July of
1928, continued for just about a year and after that, the
attractive leather-backed style disappeared. As with the
Business Coupe's portholes, the concept was to remain
dormant for 30 years or more before being revived in
the early sixties with the application of the vinyl trim to
the hardtop coupes.*

With the phasing out of the Special Coupe and its interesting leather-backed trim, the standard Coupe returned. This model was virtually identical with the Coupe first produced in November of 1927 as one of the initial six body styles. The basic body design then remained in production, essentially unchanged, through the balance of the Model A era.

1929 Type 45-A standard Coupe
John V. Allen, San Diego, California

The characteristic feature of the Coupe is the steel back. No leather or fabric trim was employed to change its appearance. Ordinarily furnished with a trunk, the rumble seat provided space for additional passengers and still offered a modified storage space.

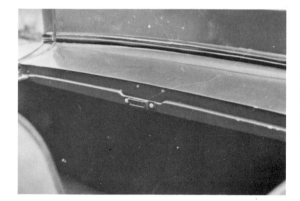

Late in the Fall of 1929, this striker plate was moved from its former position to that shown here. Note the two mounting holes of the earlier installation still punched in this car. See page 104 for comparison.

The rumble seat was available as an extra cost option on all Coupes. Not pleated, it was upholstered in artificial leather with matching side trim panels and a rubber floor mat.

The large rear window offers excellent visibility. Quarter windows and rear window do not open.

When introduced in January, there was only one 1930 Coupe, a standard model. Shortly after, though, a Deluxe Coupe was offered which differed only in the trim and in the addition of the cowl lamps and an interior dome light.

1930 Type 45-B standard Coupe   *Mr. Edgar Orange, Los Angeles, California*

Shown for comparison is the 1931 standard Coupe. The painted insert in the upper radiator shell and the one-piece splash aprons are the major differences.

The standard Coupe was not furnished with cowl lights as factory equipment.

The trunk was furnished as standard equipment on all Coupes. This could be converted to a rumble seat as an extra cost option, or even done later by the Dealer.

Spare tire cover is an accessory.

The painted windshield can be opened. In the position shown, air is directed inside and upwards under the windshield, then baffled downwards behind the belt moulding panel to provide a flow of ventilating air directed at the driver's feet.

The stripe running from the radiator to the rear and back at the bottom of the body serves to accentuate the good lines of the car.

The horn on this car is a Sparton.

No rear window frame is provided on the Coupe.

In order to remove the distinctive 1930 two-piece running board and splash apron, it is necessary to raise the body.

The fender and forward portion of the splash apron are joined to make a one-piece assembly.

A rain gutter is installed above the door.

The visor is painted, no longer fabric covered.

A vacuum windshield wiper motor is installed outside the car with its controls extending through the windshield.

A stainless steel tail light with a painted bracket is bolted to the fender.

A locking handle is provided on the curbside door.

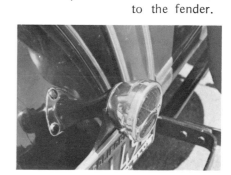

Door pockets are provided on both front doors.

A nickel-plated escutcheon plate protects the upholstery at the leveling notch.

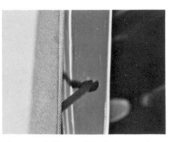

A metal door check is used on closed cars in place of a leather one used on open cars.

This leveling wedge provides a secure closing when mating with the receptacle on the edge of the door.

Note the unique brown checked cloth upholstery and the sunburst pattern of the rubber floor mat.

A trunk was standard for all Coupes although a rumble seat could have been ordered at extra cost.

The deck lid opens wide to provide access to almost 15 cubic feet of cargo space. The interior was not trimmed.

A metal stop holds the lid in the open position.

This platform, used in the rumble seat conversion is actually a necessary floor clearance for the rear spring.

Holes have been provided for the future possible installation of a rumble seat lid handle in this trunk lid.

Trunk compartments were designed for conversion to the popular rumble seat by including many of the necessary bosses and brackets. Here a lid exhibits the boss to which the lid hinge would be attached.

Also provided are the brackets to which the rumble seat hinges are to be attached.

An unusual accessory feature is the luggage rack
mounted behind the spare tire. Other accessories
seen in this view are the tire cover and center
bumper bar and the right-hand tail lamp
which had become a safety item heavily
pushed by the Dealers in late 1931.

1931 Type 45-B Deluxe Coupe   *Dr. William Ingwersen, South Gate, California*

The cowl lights and an interior dome light
were Deluxe Coupe features not shared
by the standard model.

The dashboard of the Deluxe Coupe was striped to emphasise the highlights.

Rumble seats were not a standard feature of the Coupes, but were available as an extra cost option. When installed, a metal step plate was affixed to the top of the right rear fender and another was secured to the bumper bracket.

Pockets were provided on the front doors.

The Deluxe Coupe interior is trimmed far more lavishly than that of the standard Coupe. Buttons are used to further dress up the upholstery.

The dashboard is striped on the Deluxe models.

The window garnish mouldings are finished in mahogany wood grain.

1931 Type 45-B Deluxe Coupe   *Mr. Charles Walter, Phoenix, Arizona*

Basically, all Coupes were furnished with a trunk;
the rumble seat was an optional, extra cost, item.
Trunks were fairly large, advertised as holding
"over 14 cubic feet", and were not trimmed.

Starting in June of 1931, the fixed rear window of the Coupes was offered in a version in which the glass could be lowered into a well in the rear compartment. This feature was standard on the Deluxe models, but only available at extra cost on the standard Coupe.

1931 Type 45-B standard Coupe   *Mr. Thomas Kadon, Phoenix, Arizona*

The metal visor conceals an outside-mounted vacuum windshield wiper.

179

The most popular Coupe option was undoubtedly the rumble seat. In general, this could have been ordered from the factory initially, or it could have been installed later by the Dealers. A kit was available which included all of the necessary hardware and the seat cushions, and the hinge brackets and seat platform were in the car to begin with. Most Coupes, therefore, have by now been converted to this configuration for they then offer extra passenger-carrying space.

When modified to install the rumble seat, the deck lid is not merely reversed, but the hinges and handle change their position from one end to the other of the lid.

One of the six initial models introduced, the Tudor almost immediately became the most popular of all. With a modern appearance, the enclosed car offered adequate seating for five in the comfort of a closed car. So popular was the body style that it accounted for a full 26% of all of the Model A's ever manufactured. Stated another way, one out of every four Model A's was a Tudor!

1928 Type 55-A Tudor sedan   *Mr. Glenn Johnson, Placentia, California*

All Tudor sedan bodies were built by Ford. Basically plain, the windwings, step plates, and motometer are all dress-up accessories.

The "Coupe pillar" effect also appears on the early Tudor.

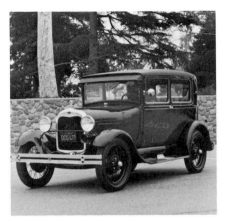

A contoured accessory trunk offered abundant space for the supplies of five passengers. The single wide door on each side of the car invited entry.

1929 Type 55-A Tudor sedan   *Mr. Don Dixon, Anaheim, California*

The visor, trimmed with top material, conceals an electric wiper. The vacuum wiper was introduced on the Tudor during the summer of 1929.

The wide doors contain pockets on their panels. A locking lever is provided on the lefthand door and an outside keylock on the right.

The rear section is steel. Only the top is fabric.

The door-pull is a part of the window moulding. Lifting the handle beneath it releases the door latch. The window handle to the right is repeated on the rear quarter windows.

The red rubber steering wheel and the center-located squeeze-grip handbrake lever are characteristic of late 1928.

To improve access, both seats can be folded as shown. However, the steering wheel prevents the driver's seat from being tipped quite as far.

The two front seats are identical. Neither is adjustable.

The rear seat is heavily padded. The back window does not lower, but the side windows do. There is a shade on the back window, but no ash tray is provided.

The 1929 Tudor was virtually identical with the 1928 model.

Attractive from all angles, the Tudor well deserved its popularity.

1929 Type 55-A Tudor sedan   *Mr. Gary Karr, Scottsdale, Arizona*

The upper part of the body of this car is painted the same color as the mouldings. Others have this panel painted to match the lower body color. Either is correct.

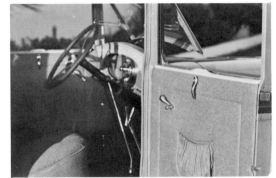

This car is dated 1-2-29. It is still equipped with the squeeze-grip hand brake lever.

To provide a more pleasing appearance, the top line of the window does not follow the roof line.

The 1928 style tail lamp was used on this very early 1929 car.

This redesigned Tudor was introduced in January of 1930. Still produced only as a standard Tudor, there seemed little to talk about, but Ford found a way. By slightly shortening the depth of the rear seat, it was claimed that the new model now had "increased passenger space in the rear seat".

From the cowl back, the car appeared to be unchanged from its previous version. However, by smoothly fairing the cowl and eliminating the Coupe pillar, and by lowering the body on smaller, 19", wheels, the effect was that of a whole new design and Ford went on to build over 425,000 of this model in 1930, almost 30% of that year's entire production.

Less exotic than some of the body types, less sporty than others, and perhaps even less attractive than most, the Tudor sedan provided the nucleus around which the entire Model A program was built.

1930 Type 55-B Tudor sedan   *Mr. Maynard Talley, Tucson, Arizona*

When viewed from this angle, it is difficult quickly to determine whether the car is a 1928-29 or a 1930-31 but for the 19" wheels, which with their larger hubcaps, and their lowering effect, make the car appear wider.

No cowl lamps were furnished with the Tudor sedans. However, in common with all other 1930 bodies, the front wooden stringer was pre-drilled to receive them.

Produced only during the last half of 1931, the Deluxe Tudor appears to have been a last-ditch effort by Ford to bolster sagging sales by offering a more luxurious-appearing car. With cowl lamps, dome lights, and a dressed-up interior trim, including an adjustable driver's seat and floor carpets, the car nevertheless remained basically a Tudor sedan.

1931 Type 55-B Deluxe Tudor sedan   *Mr. David Crook, Scottsdale, Arizona*

The cowl lamps are standard on the 1931 Deluxe Tudor sedan.

Whitewall tires, center bumper bar, and spare tire lock are accessories.

Little about the 1928-29 Tudor seems to
have changed in this view of the
1931 Deluxe Tudor.

An accessory keylock and locking
strap protect the spare wheel.

The center bumper bar is an accessory,
well regarded for protection of
the spare wheel.

The smoothly faired cowl section offers
a modern look which still retains
its good appearance.

Unlike the standard Tudor sedan which was provided with rubber mats, the Deluxe Tudor had a brown carpet in both the front and the rear. As with other deluxe models, the dashboard is striped.

In common with other late 1931 models, the firewall is indented for the fuel shut-off. A vacuum line from the intake manifold is used to operate the windshield wipers.

Cowl lamps were furnished only on the 1931 Deluxe Tudor. Those Tudors manufactured prior to June of that year were standards, and did not enjoy this feature unless by special order for the accessory.

This locking handle is provided on the righthand front door.

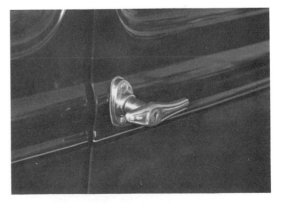

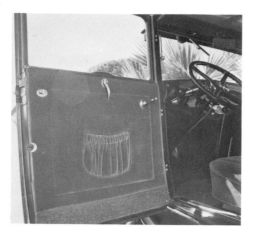

A new feature, first used on the Deluxe Tudor, is this use of the floor carpet at the bottom of the doors and rear seat panels.

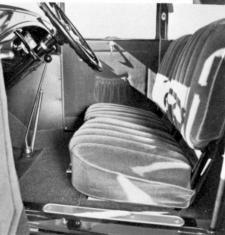

The driver's seat is now on an adjustable track. Its back folds, but better access to the rear seat is obtained at the passenger's seat which not only folds as shown, but also tips forward.

Although the pull-down shade appears in standard Tudors, the addition of the dome light is unique to the Deluxe Tudor sedan.

A new feature on the Deluxe Tudor is the arm rest on either side of the rear seat.

1929 Type 60-B Fordor Sedan   *Mr. Jack Athey, Oceanside, California*

Although a Fordor sedan had been announced with the others on December 1, 1927, the car then depicted apparently never was produced! As shown in what must have been an artist's sketch, the Fordor was to have had three windows, and a distinct coupe pillar. For reasons now obscure, the body style was not produced, and although prices had been announced, (and presumably orders had been taken), the first Fordor sedan, this two-window style did not appear until May of 1928.

With a Briggs-built body, the design was a true departure from the other body styles. The coupe pillar had been eliminated, and the gas tank, which forms a visible part of the body in the earlier design, was now concealed beneath the smoothly flowing fairing giving the car a more modern look. This styling was to become the standard for all of the 1930-31 body styles.

The earliest of these Fordor sedans featured a cowl ventilator placed just forward of the lower door hinge, and a celluloid visor. These features were eliminated shortly, but the brown leather-back trim was retained, and then joined by 1929 by a black leather-back (60-B), and a painted steel back (60-C).

Wheels have been repainted,
were originally black.

The smoothly flowing lines of the cowl are clear in this view. The coupe pillar has been eliminated.

Three versions of this car, Types 60-A (brown leather), 60-B (black leather), and 60-C (steel back), differ only in the treatment of the upper back panels.

Doors open from the center, and access to either compartment is quite good.

No cowl lights distract from the smooth
appearance of the new cowl section.

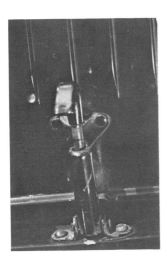

This is the "early" style hood cleat having
three mounting holes. Compare with the
"later" style on page 99.

The visor is covered with the same material as the top, either brown or black artificial leather.

A painted electric windshield wiper motor is mounted under the visor.

Characteristic of the Briggs bodies is the flat upper edge of the window glass and the correspondingly squared-off look of the door frame. Note that unlike the Tudor (pg 186), the roof line is quite flat above the door.

The graceful lines of the early door handles flow in a symmetrical pattern. The ends of both handles point downwards.

The body overhangs the splash apron at the rear.

A skirt is furnished at the bottom
rear of the body.

The sedans are wider and thus
have narrower fenders.

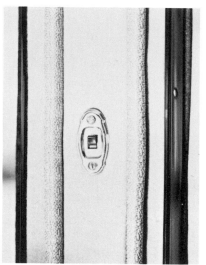

An interior dome light is placed over the rear window and is operated by a switch installed in the right pillar.

The nickel-plated door pull is a separate part fastened to the door moulding.

The inside door handles were nickel-plated although most were satin-finished rather than bright.

1929 Type 60-A Fordor sedan   *Mr. Larry Caskey, Pomona, California*

This brown leather-back Fordor sedan, dated
1-22-29 on its firewall, still has the drum
tail lamp as does the slightly later (2-29)
Type 60-B on page 193.

The rectangular window opening, characteristic of the Briggs bodies, is emphasised by the manner in which the frames are painted.

Briggs bodies front doors are wider than their rear doors. The front door is 28 ¼" wide, while the rear measures only 26 ¾", a difference of one and a half inches.

Most, but not all, early cars were stamped with a date on their lower left panel of the fuel tank. This date, generally accepted as the assembly date here appears as 1 22 29.

The distinctive rear quarter of the 1929
Type 60 two-window Fordor sedan.

This is the upper rear corner of the 1929
Type 60 two-window Fordor sedan.

In July of 1929, Briggs introduced *another*
two-window Fordor sedan which was
fundamentally the three-window
model with the rear quarter closed.
This type, designated Type 170, has
a slightly wider rear quarter.

The distinctive rear quarter of the 1929
Type 170 two-window Fordor sedan.

Introduced in July of 1929, the Type 170 Fordor
sedan was carried over into 1930 with a redesigned
cowl and otherwise essentially unchanged. A fairly
plain model, having no cowl lights, and a simple
interior, an upgrading to a Deluxe Fordor sedan
followed shortly after March of 1930.

1930 Type 170 Fordor sedan   *Mr. Richard Allen, Carlsbad, California*

The tire cover and right hand
tail light are accessories.

The two-window Fordor sedan, Type 170-A,
when introduced in July of 1928, did not
have cowl lamps, nor did its 1930 version.

The Type 170-B Deluxe Fordor sedan was introduced in April of 1930 and carried through for about one year. It was more luxuriously upholstered than the earlier standard Fordor, and was equipped with the popular cowl lamps.

After April of 1931, the Type 170-B Deluxe Fordor was replaced with the new slant-windshield Deluxe Fordor, the Type 160-C, another, and final, two-window Fordor sedan.

Trimmed with deluxe features, the Type 170-B now has cowl lamps as standard equipment.

Whitewall tires, windwings, step plate, and motometer are all accessories as is the rear center bumper bar.

1930 Type 170-B Deluxe Fordor sedan   *Mr. Joe H. Clary, Anaheim, California*

An accessory spare tire guard protects the rear wheel.

Compare handles with those on page 196.

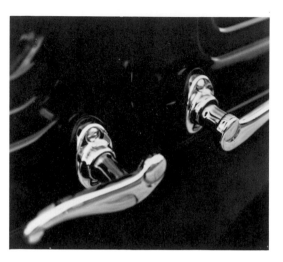

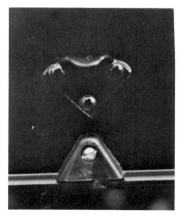

The 1930-31 hoods are equipped with a triangular cleat rather than the half-round style used earlier.

Door pockets are furnished on the rear doors only. All doors have locking levers.

The square corners and the flat upper lines
of the Briggs-built bodies are evident in
this view. The garnish mouldings are
painted mahogany.

A center arm rest is provided in the
rear seat in addition to the side
rests. This is a deluxe feature
shared only with the Town Sedan.

A dome light is placed above the rear
window, and a pull-down window
shade can be used to increase privacy.

The interior shown here is original
and has not been replaced.

1930 Deluxe Fordor sedan   1931 standard Coupe

White sidewall tires, windwings,
and step plates are accessories.

1929 Type 165-B Fordor sedan
Mr. Arnold Friend, Phoenix, Arizona

The original black factory-issue
wheels have been repainted.

Starting in January of 1929, Ford offered a new, three-window Fordor sedan in addition to the earlier two-window Fordor. This new model then carried forward virtually unchanged until the Spring of 1931 when it was succeeded by the slant windshield model. From its introduction until it was replaced, the basic body was unchanged except as required to adapt the 1930-31 cowl.

The Fordor was considered a "standard" model, and came with little in the way of deluxe appointments. These were reserved for use in the similar deluxe model known as the Town Sedan which is alike in all ways but for trim and accessories.

Although Briggs had been the exclusive builders of the two-window Fordor sedans, these new models were built by both Briggs and also Murray. Their bodies, designed to the same standards, and interchangeable as a whole, did not however contain many interchangeable components.

This smoothly faired cowl section, lacking the coupe pillar of the other early body styles, is identical to the same section of the two-window Fordor sedan (pg 195). Employed exclusively on the Fordor sedans, it became part of the basic design of all 1930-31 models.

The moulding carried forward to the radiator and provided a quite pleasing effect.

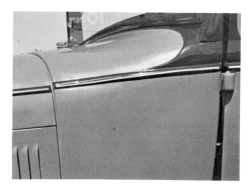

No cowl lights were furnished with the Fordor which was the "standard" version of this body style. The deluxe version was known as the Town Sedan.

The windshield is painted upper
body color which is the same
from the belt moulding up.

The interior of the Fordor sedan is quite stark.
The rear window is provided with a shade,
but there are no pleats in the seats.

A dome light is furnished, but the back
quarter windows can not be opened.

The windwings and the white sidewall tires are accessories.

1931 Type 160-A Fordor sedan   *Mr. Albert Swinscoe, Fallbrook, California*

Introduced in May of 1931, the Type 160-A Fordor sedan is the "standard" of the slant-windshield series, and thus has no cowl lights. The spare wheel is rear-mounted, and the interior is upholstered with no center arm rest and far less extravagance than the Town Sedan which it greatly resembles.

The rear quarter windows can be lowered in this model, but the interior woodgraining trim of the deluxe models has been replaced with a maroon painted finish.

1929 Town Sedan
Type 155-B
Body by Briggs

1929 Fordor
Type 165-B
Body by Briggs

The Town Sedan, Type 155-A (body by Murray), and Type 155-B (body by Briggs), was the more popular of the body types. Whether the Town Sedan was a "dressed-up" Fordor sedan, or whether the three-window Fordor sedan was a stripped-down Town Sedan is not entirely clear, but, judging by the numerical sequence of the Type numbers, it would appear that the latter was the case. Certainly the stark Fordor suffered by comparison to the deluxe features of the Town Sedan.

This same body was used, with the necessary cowl section modifications, on the 1930 and early 1931 three-window Fordor sedans before being discontinued in May of 1931.

1929 Type 155-B Town Sedan   *Mr. Dan Nowlin, Phoenix, Arizona*

Type 155-A Town Sedan
Body by Murray

Type 155-B Town Sedan
Body by Briggs

The upper line of the door frame, around the window glass, is quite flat, a characteristic of the Briggs bodies.

As with all Fordor sedans, the cowl is smoothly faired, and lacks the abrupt coupe pillar of other early models.

Cowl lights are furnished as standard equipment on the Town Sedan. They are the significant external difference between it and the three-window Fordor sedan.

This Town Sedan, with body by Briggs, has pockets on both front doors, and an additional set on the rear doors (below).

The interior shown here is original and has not been replaced.

A dome light is provided over the rear window which is equipped with a pull-down shade as are the quarter windows. None of these windows can be opened.

A pull-down center arm rest is provided in the Town Sedan, and seats are upholstered with attractive pleats.

Two end arm rests and the center rest provide relaxing travel for two passengers, or, by raising the center rest, accommodations for three rear seat passengers.

The windshield swings open for ventilation. A nickel-plated door pull is fastened to the window moulding.

Note the square lines of the door jamb above the rear window (left), and the front (right). This is typical of the Briggs-built Fordor bodies. The front doors on these Briggs bodies are over one inch wider than the rear ones (see tapes below).

1929 Type 155-B Town Sedan
Body by Briggs
White sidewall tires are
an accessory.

These two Town Sedans are quite similar in appearance. Note, however, the arch of the top of the windows on the Murray body (below), and the fact that the doors on the Briggs bodies are of different width.

This same body was used, with only the necessary cowl section modifications, in 1930 and early 1931.

1929 Type 155-A Town Sedan
Body by Murray

Mr. Dan Miller, Downey, California

1929 Type 155-A Town Sedan
Body by Murray

Mr. Robert Curwin, San Diego, California

Although resembling the Briggs body from a distance, the Murray body had some distinct differences making component parts largely non-interchangeable. Among these differences were the fact that on the Murray bodies, doors were of the same width, and a more obvious difference is the appearance of the top lines of the windows which in the Murray bodies were gracefully arched.

This Murray Body Company identification plate is affixed to the lower righthand cowl section.

From their introduction in 1929, through early 1931, the three-window Fordor sedan bodies were unchanged (other than the necessary cowl section modifications in 1930). Those bodies built by Briggs differed greatly from those built by Murray although superficially they appeared to be alike.

In March of 1931, a **new** three-window Fordor was introduced, the "slant windshield" Fordor. Built by **both** Murray and Briggs to identical design, they represent the "top of the line" in Model A design.

The line again included a standard Fordor sedan, Type 160-A, and a dressed-up, deluxe, version called the Town Sedan, Type 160-B. It is unclear whether one was to be a "dressed-up" Fordor, or the other was a "stripped-down" Town Sedan, but the effect is the same.

1931 Type 160-B Town Sedan   *Mr. Richard Krist, Orange, California*

Type 160-B Town Sedan
Body by Briggs

The principal identifying feature of the "slant-windshield" cars is this backward-sloping area.

The slanted windshield also opens out from the bottom for increased ventilation.

Although the single, rear-mounted spare wheel was standard, many slant-windshield Town Sedans were purchased with dual side-mounted spares for a heightened deluxe appearance.

There is no visor on slant-windshield cars. The windwing is an accessory.

An accessory luggage rack, and frequently a trunk, is generally found mounted at the rear of those cars with the optional side mounts. Another common accessory is the right-hand tail light.

The arch of the top of the center window suggests Murray, but actually both Murray *and* Briggs built the slant-windshield sedans, and their products are indistinguishable.

The rear quarter windows can now be opened for ventilation, a new feature, introduced on the slant windshield sedans.

On *this* car, the doors have no pockets, but a single large pocket appears on the back of the front seat,

This interior is done in brown mohair. While the
earliest of the Town Sedans had contained a
center arm rest, this was soon eliminated.
A T-headed handle operates the glass
in the quarter window.

A robe rail is provided, and a large single
pocket with a flap is placed on the
back of the front seat.

Although there is no pocket on either
front door, or on the left kick panel,
there *is* one on the right side kick panel.

These luxurious pleated seats of a
Town Sedan contrast with the
plain trim of a standard Fordor.

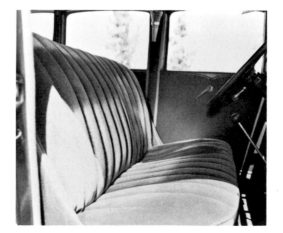

The keylock is now contained within the front right-hand door handle, an innovation since previously it had been placed beneath it.

Two sun visors are provided.

Curiously, the sun visors are hinged at their rear edge and thus tend to be placed uncomfortably close to the passengers' faces.

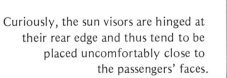

The interior shown here is original and has not been replaced.

An accessory tire cover decorates the standard rear-mounted spare wheel of this Town Sedan.

1931 Type 160-B Town Sedan

Mr. Vernon Bayer, Mesa, Arizona

In contrast with another 1931 slant-windshield Town Sedan reviewed previously on page 221, this car has door pockets on all four doors. There does not appear, however, to be any correlation between this difference and the body manufacturer though.

This door has a pocket. Contrast this view with that of a similar original car on page 222.

Within any given body type and model year, variations did exist. On this page, and on page 222 are seen interior studies of two "identical" Type 160-B Town Sedans, both original.

In one case, there are four door pockets; in the other, none. One car has an unusual, large, pocket on the back of the front seat, the other none.

The large pocket on the back of the front seat (pg 222) is omitted but the robe rail remains.

The rear window shade has a pull-tab rather than the tassel found in a similar car (pg 221).

The interior shown here is original and has not been replaced.

1931

The Victoria, one of Model A's most attractive versions, was introduced late in November of 1930 and was produced through to the end of the line. It was a truly deluxe car offering many unique features, among them the little bustle back with an enclosed storage space behind the front seat.

Offered in the steel-top version shown here, the Victoria was also available through April of 1931 in a leather-backed style in which a two-tone tan artificial leather covered the top and the back quarter.

There appears to have been little difference between the 1930 model, first available in November, and the 1931 since all were produced with the typical 1931 radiator shell.

1931 Type 190-A Victoria   *Mr. Bill Vaughn, Orange, California*

The rear-mounted spare tire is hung at a steeper angle than on other models.

The bustle, a characteristic of the Victoria, conceals a storage space entered from the interior of the car.

The wide single door makes for an easy access to the interior. The side and rear quarter windows can be opened, but the back window is fixed.

The right-hand tail lamp is an accessory. By late 1931, Ford was exhorting all of its Dealers to sell this safety item.

The front seats fold, and the passenger seat also tilts forward for better access to the rear. The driver's seat is adjustable (see handle in lower photo), and the inside door handles are a new style that rotate to release the latch.

The pleated rear seat back tilts forward to expose the storage compartment within the bustle.

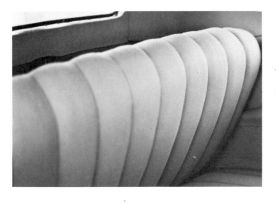

The roof of the Victoria has been lowered for design effect, and to provide adequate headroom, the floor has also been depressed.

The mahogany-painted window garnish moulding is missing in this car.

Cowl lights are standard on the Victoria, a deluxe model. No sun visor is provided.

In late 1931, a running change was made which saw the introduction of this bracket which supports the steering column from the underside of the belt moulding. This change was made on all late 1931 cars and finally answered the problem of the gas tank leaks caused by the previous bracket. The accessory oil pressure gage below the conventional instrument panel is a Ford accessory.

1931 Type 400-A Convertible Sedan   *Mr. David Treichel, South Gate, California*

The Convertible Sedan was produced in extremely limited numbers. Introduced quite late in Model A production, in May of 1931, only about 5000 in all were built. Popular as much for its sporty appearance as for its deluxe trim, the car offered up to five passengers the comfort of a closed car and the pleasure of an open model.

The fender-mounted spare wheel was standard for this model adding to the deluxe effect. The radiator stone guard, headlamp visors, and hood side panels are accessories as are the quail and outside mirror.

The canvas top is held in place by seven snap fasteners on each side. The body is depressed at the rear to allow the folded top to lie almost horizontally. The windwings are accessories.

The framework over the door and around the quarter window remains in place when the top is lowered thus offering an entirely different view than that of the Deluxe Phaeton.

To add to its appearance as a closed car, the top is constructed in such a way that the canvas conceals the metal and wood frame.

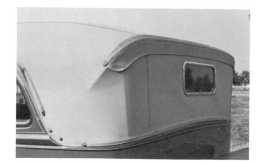

These more modern inside door handles which rotate to release the latch were introduced in the 1931 slant windshield models replacing the earlier lift-to-open style.

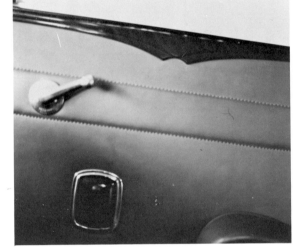

The rear quarter windows of the Convertible Sedan could be lowered by turning these conveniently located window cranks. Two ash trays, one on each side, were provided, the first Ford model to have this feature.

Two thumbscrews lock the front header in position when the top is raised.

This chromed latching assembly is used to give added rigidity to the top of the Convertible Sedan. A leather strap (lower right corner of picture) places tension on the bow giving the top a quite solid appearance.

An extra canvas flap is sewn around the painted rear window frame on the inside and fastened with three snap fasteners to the seat back for additional top support.

In addition to the accessory luggage rack and metal trunk, the most striking feature in this view is the full-width rear bumper which was standard on the Convertible Sedan and Deluxe Phaeton.

The Model A Taxicab is one of the most rare of all models. Produced in only one version starting in late 1928, about 5000 were manufactured in 1929, and after only 275 more were made in 1930, it was discontinued.

The basic limitation of seating only four, rather than the conventional five passengers found in competing models, was probably the largest single factor in the lack of acceptance of the Model A taxicab. For example, in New York City, where the law **required** *the taxicabs to accommodate five passengers, the Model A Taxicab was not granted a license for operation on application in June of 1929. Not until almost two years of arguments had elapsed was the Ford taxicab to be permitted on the streets of New York City. Then, in February of 1931, six Ford taxicabs were placed into operation briefly there, but by then, the damage had already been done.*

The Taxicab is the only four door sedan resembling the Fordor announced initially. All other Fordors were built with a smoothly faired cowl section but the Taxicab was produced with the sharply defined front pillar at the cowl.

1929 Type 135-A Taxicab   *Mr. John Greenland, Allston, Massachusetts*

With a partition dividing the front and rear compartments, the Taxicab was designed to seat a fourth rear compartment passenger by recessing a folding jump seat into the forward compartment. The small space forward of that was used for luggage, parcels, and for the calibrating Taximeter. The interior was nicely upholstered, but the rear quarter windows did not open. By September of 1929, a handle had been installed just forward of the rear window crank to enable passengers to pull the door shut rather than by grasping the lowered window glass and perhaps breaking it.

Resembling a similar view of the 1929 three-window Fordor, the Taxicab has somewhat more square quarter windows, lacks a skirt at the rear of the body, and displays the sharp edge of the cowl pillar. Using 4:75 x 21 tires, larger than normal, the Taxicab required a larger locking spare wheel tire band than other models.

The 1929 Town Car, not to be confused with the Town Sedan, was Ford's challenge to the luxury automobile market. It was, however, a misdirected challenge because the body style was never accepted by the public. Only about 1200 of these unusual cars were ever built, all but about 200 in 1929. With the enclosed rear compartment, an air of class distinction was suggested. However, the Ford automobile had itself earned its association with the common man, and the attempt to upgrade its image was soon abandoned.

1929 Type 140-A Town Car   *Mr. John Greenland, Allston, Massachusetts*

The lamps placed above and between the doors are carriage lamps not found on the original Town Car, and the fender-mounted spare wheels and rear-mounted luggage are accessories along with the white sidewall tires. As originally conceived, the Town Car has a rear-mounted single spare wheel.

Priced at $1200, the top of the Ford line, at a time when the Roadster was offered at $435 and the Fordor sedans at $600, the Town Car was a deliberate attempt to strike at the luxury market. When further "dressed up" with the accessory side mounts shown on this car, its appeal was improved, but the prominent radiator and cowl still advertise it as "merely" a Model A Ford.

The interior of the car is upholstered in a deluxe mohair material, but the open air chaffeur's compartment is done in leather. A removable leather canopy was furnished to be snapped over the front seat compartment in the event of inclement weather. A sliding glass partition separates the enclosed rear compartment.

The 1929 Station Wagon· was the first such body to be produced by Ford. Earlier, similar bodies (known as "Depot Hacks") had been fitted to Model T chassis as early as 1912 by commercial body shops, but until the introduction, in January of 1929 of the newly named "Station Wagon", these were always custom bodies.

1929 Type 150-A Station Wagon   *Mr. William Lyons, Costa Mesa, California*

The typical metal cowl is enhanced by the look of the all-wood body.

Truly box-like in appearance, the lines of the Station Wagon are very square.

Mounting the 21" spare wheel in the left front fender meant notching the wood to allow the driver's door clearance for opening.

Body structural members are made of maple; the panels are birch. All door hinges are enclosed piano-type.

The rows of fasteners are employed to hold the canvas side curtains.

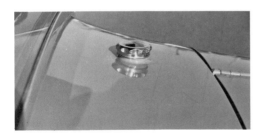

Curved wooden sections are joined to provide an interesting fender line.

1929 Type 49-A Special Coupe   *Mr. Eugene Show, San Diego, California*

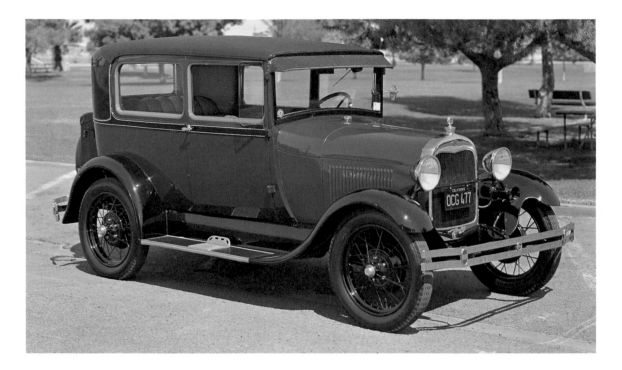

1928 Type 55-A Tudor sedan   *Mr. Don Dixon, Anaheim, California*

1931 Type 55-B Deluxe Tudor sedan   *Mr. David Crook, Scottsdale, Arizona*

1929 Type 60-B Fordor sedan   *Mr. John W. Athey, Oceanside, California*

1930 Type 170-B Deluxe Fordor sedan   *Mr. Joe H. Clary, Anaheim, California*

1928 Type 155-B Town Sedan   *Mr. Dan Nowlin, Phoenix, Arizona*

1931 Type 160-B Town Sedan   *Mr. Richard Krist, Fullerton, California*

1929 Type 150-A Station Wagon   *Mr. William Lyons, Costa Mesa, California*

1931 Type 190-A Victoria   *Mr. Bill Vaughn, Orange, California*

1928 Type 76-A open cab Pick-up　　　　*Mr. Joe C. Pittman, Phoenix, Arizona*

1931 Type 76-B open cab Pick-up　　　　*Mr. Arthur C. Edwardson, Phoenix, Arizona*

1929 Type 78-A closed cab Pick-up *Mr. J. R. Draskovich, Oxnard, California*

1928 Type 188-A Stake Truck *Mr. Max Herman, Flintridge, California*

247

1929 Type 68-A Convertible Cabriolet *Mr. Carroll Vaughn, Jr., No. Hollywood, California*

1929 Type 54-A Business Coupe *Mr. Delbert Pantel, Chico, California*

The windshield frame is
painted body color.

An outside rear view mirror
is standard on this model.

The Station Wagon, like other commercial models,
was produced in only two styles. The first was
manufactured from introduction through June of
1930, and the "later" style from then on.
A characteristic of the earlier style is this sun
visor which was deleted on the later model.

Unlike the other commercial models with
their painted radiator shell and lamps,
the Station Wagon has the conventional
nickeled front end appearance.

Two individual seats are placed just inside the rear doors. These seats can be tilted forward as needed.

The door locks are fastened over the inside door paneling.

A narrow, but passable, aisle is provided between the two individual seats to allow access to the far rear bench seat.

The door handles are nickel-plated.

The roof is made of a series of slats supported by a wooden framework and covered with artificial leather.

The tail gate can easily be lowered in order to carry luggage or parcels.

When lowered, the tail gate is supported by two leather-sheathed chains. If not supported, it will hang free.

A metal compartment built in under the floor, and accessible from the rear, is provided for the storage of the side curtains.

The rear seat assembly is removable to provide extra storage space within the body. It also may be tilted forward when required.

The rear mounting legs of the rear seat fit into these receptacles recessed into the floor.

Hinges, brackets, and other hardware are painted black.

The snap fasteners for the rear quarter side curtains are *inside* the roof support. Water washing down the roof would thus fall outside the curtain.

The door hinges are of continuous piano-style. The rear door, just forward of the hinge in this view, has side curtain fasteners secured to the outside.

All body hardware such as this rear tail gate latch, the upper corner gussets (above), the strap hinges on the tail gate (right), and other similar pieces are painted black along with the conventional black running gear and wheels.

The Model A Station Wagon, a product of the commercial line, was manufactured in only two versions, the 1929 style being carried into June of 1930. Then, starting in July of that year, the "new" version shown here was placed into production, and carried through to the end of the Model A line.

1931 Type 150-B Station Wagon   *Mr. Charles Peters, Whittier, California*

Shown for comparison is the earlier Type 150-A of 1929.

The sun visor, a characteristic of the earlier style has now been eliminated

The door handles are now made of rustless steel. These are generally installed so that ends point downward.

The side curtain snap fasteners are now placed *outside* the rear quarter opening, a change from the earlier style.

Snap fasteners are provided to hold the canvas side curtains. Bodies are made of maple with birch paneling.

The body hardware which in the earlier model had been black, is now painted Manila Brown, a color which blends more attractively with the wooden body.

The seating arrangement is unchanged. The narrow aisle between the individual seats is retained. A framing member has been added at the rear quarter window to provide a mounting for the canvas side curtains.

The tail light is supported under the body by a unique bracket.

The door panels are wood-lined, and a rubber mat is used in both the front and rear compartments. As with the earlier model, seats are removable for extra cargo space.

Following the change to smaller wheels on the later style is the change in the design of the left front door on the Station Wagons. While the earlier door had to be notched (see below) to allow for clearance of the larger wheel, the later style could be built without this feature thus allowing for a more pleasing appearance.

Section of 1929-30 Station Wagon shown here for comparison.

The steel quarter "window" is wider than that of the Tudor which it resembles (page181).

The Deluxe Delivery was introduced in late 1929, and offered commercial users an enclosed maximum volume storage body on a passenger car chassis. Featuring a large rear-entry door, the car resembled the Tudor sedan, but with the rear quarter windows closed in. In actuality, such was not the case as the rear section is a design unique to this body style.

The rear door is hinged to
open from the curb side
for easiest loading.

Very evident is this typical coupe pillar.
The rear view mirror is standard for
commercial models, but the step
plates are accessories.

A locking rear door handle
is provided.

A rain gutter is installed
over the rear door.

The visor is covered with top material.
The outside rear view mirror is
standard on commercial models.

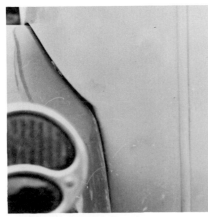

The body folds uniquely
over the fender.

1928 Type 76-A open cab Pick-Up   *Mr. Joseph Pittman, Phoenix, Arizona*

The Pick-Up was introduced as a commercial vehicle late in 1928. Employing a black-painted radiator shell rather than the plated one, and similar headlamps, it even lacked a rear bumper. The running boards were steel and had no rubber covering.

Originally the mark of a commercial vehicle, the fender-mounted spare was provided to make the rear more accessible. The windwing is an accessory.

With the side curtains snapped into place, the cab is quite comfortable.

The design clearly shows the prominent coupe pillar.

Similarly to the very early open passenger cars, there are no outside door handles.

An inside door latch, easily reached from the outside, is provided with a nickeled knob.

The pick-up box greatly resembled that of the earlier Model T. The back window is Isinglass, sewn directly into the fabric top.

The upholstery is plain artificial
leather, and is not pleated.

Unlike the previous Model T which employed a
gusset to flow the Roadster body into the
lines of the box, the "square" corner of
the back of this cab appears to have been designed
to allow for maximum hauling space.

The top support structure is composed of
painted metal straps, sockets, and wooden
bows. This mechanism is rigid, and will not fold.

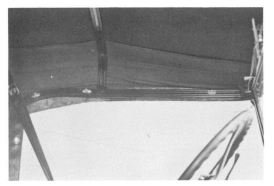

A leather-sheathed chain supports
the lowered tailgate.

The sides of the metal pick-up box are topped by flared sections to accommodate side-boards for an increase in carrying capacity.

The fenders are secured to the sides of the pick-up box and ride high over the wheel in an unloaded pick-up.

The back of the cab is designed so that it can be used with other commercial bodies as well as the Pick-Up, the box for which is a separate entity. The bolts seen on the back of the cab are used to secure the back of the seat frame.

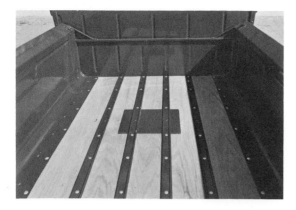

Pick-Up beds are factory painted, the wood having received a coat of primer, and the bed then painted as an assembly. This example has been finished as shown to emphasise the use of the wood floor.

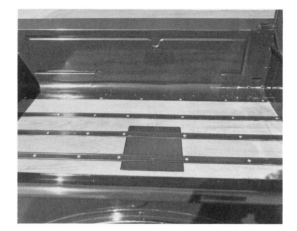

The metal plate in the center of the bed, covers the rear cross-member and the spring center bolt. Differing from the earlier Model T pick-up box which it resembles, there is now no access plate at the forward left part of the bed for the battery which has now been moved to a position at the driver's feet.

The side-board sockets at the corners of the bed are located differently in Model T pick-ups where they are inset along the sides away from the corners.

Early items such as this red rubber steering wheel which was discontinued in the passenger cars late in 1928, were often carried on into the commercial line until supplies were used up.

A rubber floor mat is provided.

The pick-up box is fastened to the chassis with eight bolts, four on each side. Between the bed and the chassis is a wooden stringer. The box is fastened to the stringer alone with the rear two of the eight bolts.

1928-29 Type 76-A Pick-Up

Production of the earlier style continued into June of 1930 at which time a newly-designed open pick-up was made available. Similar in appearance, the later design had the same box, but the forward compartment was redesigned to eliminate the coupe pillar, and to otherwise update the vehicle.

1930-31 Type 76-B Pick-Up

Introduced in June of 1930, this design has more rounded corners at the rear of the passenger compartment.

1930 Type 76-B Pick-Up *Mr. Arthur Edwardson, Phoenix, Arizona*

The black-painted radiator shell and headlights are furnished in their new configuration.

No cowl lights are furnished on this commercial vehicle.

The isinglass rear window is
sewn directly into the top.

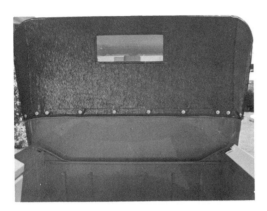

New this year is a feature which permits the
entire top (which is non-folding) to be
removed from the cab. Snap fasteners at
the rear are loosened, and two prop nuts
above the windshield released, and the
entire assembly lifts off.

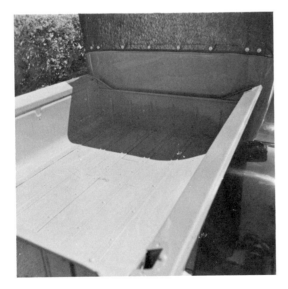

The pick-up bed is painted
body color.

With the top removed, the design
has come to be recognized as an
exceptionally sporty one.

The top is non-folding, but removable. The windshield stanchions now fold, a new feature, and the windshield can thus be laid almost flat on the cowl. The windwings are accessories.

An accessory right rear tail light is held by a bracket fastened under the bed. The body of the light is painted black.

Outside door handles are supplied on this model. There is, however, no keylock furnished.

The windshield frame and stanchions are painted black along with the radiator shell and the lights.

The pick-up bed rests on two
wooden stringers which are
secured to the chassis with
the same bolts that hold
the bed on.

This view of the underside of the bed shows
the metal stringers to which the wooden
slats of the bed are secured.

The accessory spring covers are used
to keep water and road dirt out of
the springs. The tailpipe of the
Model A passes over the radius rod
and *under* the rear axle.

The closed cab Pick-Up was introduced in 1928, and while it appeared to be a totally new design, it actually was a clever mating of many Model T parts with the Model A chassis and cowl. Square and austere in appearance, the closed cab Pick-Up provided commercial users with an all-weather, reliable, light-duty truck.

1929 Type 78-A closed cab Pick-Up   *Mr. J.R. Draskovich, Oxnard, California*

Model A welled front fenders were introduced on these commercial models to improve the access to the rear. Earlier, the similar Model T carried its spare under the back of the bed.

The steel back of the closed cab is reinforced by stamped channels. The outside rear view mirror is standard for commercial types.

The tailgate lowers to extend the length of the bed and to ease loading heavy objects.

An embossed rear quarter panel adds to the effect, but was never punctured to provide windows. This model, with roll-up windows, was supplied with door handles.

The bed is identical to that furnished on the open cab Pick-Up model.

The square lines of the closed cab Pick-Up assume a pleasing appearance in this view.

Roll-up windows provide the comforts of a closed car. The nickeled inside door knob, similar to that used on early open cars, is still employed on this 1929 commercial vehicle.

The visor is covered with top material. A black-painted vacuum wiper is installed on this vehicle; originally, a hand-operated wiper was furnished.

The windshield may be pivoted open for increased ventilation.

The commercial rear view mirror is placed outside on an arm long enough to clear the load. It is mounted to the door frame.

Commercial line vehicles were furnished with all-steel running boards unlike those on the passenger cars. They bear a non-skid diamond pattern, and are marked with the familiar Ford script (below).

The embossed steel center panel of the cab back has a self-contained window frame.

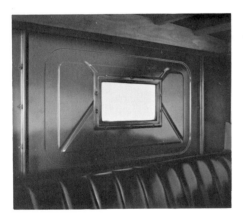

A metal pocket is provided on each side of the cab to contain maps, delivery order books, etc.

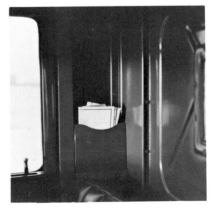

The outside door handles have a black insert trim panel. A keylock is provided beneath the handle on the curbside door.

The nickeled inside door knob is similar to that used on the 1928 open cars.

The door pulls are formed by embossing the garnish moulding.

To heighten effect, the wood in this restored car has been varnished. Originally it was painted body color along with the rest of the bed.

Introduced in June of 1930 was a newly styled closed cab Pick-Up, Type 82-B. Featuring a smoothly faired cowl section similar to the passenger cars of that year, and a rounded back on the cab, the design brought a modernity that was to survive for years to come. The pick-up box remained unchanged for the next year and continued to be adaptable to side-boards, racks, and canopies.

1930 Type 82-B closed cab Pick-Up   *Mr. Donald Clark, Santa Ana, California*

The black-painted radiator shell and headlamps are characteristic of the Ford commercial line.

This 1931 Pick-Up has an accessory stainless steel radiator shell
and headlamps. The wheels, however, were optionally painted
in one of several different colors. The commercial line
continued to use the two-piece splash aprons long
after they were discontinued on the passenger cars.

The 19" wheel sits lower in the
later well than does the larger
earlier 21" tire.

The larger rear window of the 1930-31 Pick-Up contrasts
with the small one on the 1928-29 style (page 271).
The pick-up box is identical though.

Presenting an entirely new appearance, the rear quarter
of the 1930-31 Pick-Up is markedly different than the
earlier style. Smoothly rounded, and with a larger
window, the back now curves both at the sides and the
top to provide a far more modern appearance.

The coupe pillar has been eliminated, and the cowl fairs smoothly into the body. No sidelights are furnished on these commercial models.

This rear-view mirror is supported by the hinge pin, not fastened to the body itself.

Small round head rivets replace the larger fasteners on the earlier hinge strap (page 275).

The wood in the original pick-up bed was painted along with the rest of the body. Restorers frequently varnish the wood for heightened effect.

In August of 1931, a new all-steel closed cab Pick-Up with its body manufactured by Budd was introduced by Ford. This was especially notable as it was the first all-steel automobile body to be produced by any company, and it would not be until 1937, almost eight years later, that Ford was to make the all-steel body the standard method of building automobiles.

1931 Type 82-B closed cab Pick-Up   *Tim & Bill Sharon, South Pasadena, California*

Virtually identical to the fabric-topped closed cab Pick-Up, this view shows little difference from the earlier style.

Starting in about May of 1931, a new, larger all-steel pick-up box became available. This box had a steel floor, and was a bit higher, extending almost to the belt line of the cab. The side-boards are added accessories.

Viewed from above, the all-steel roof panel is quite evident. Steel ribs, rather than wood, reinforce the top.

The windwings are accessories, but the rear-view mirror was standard on commercial models. Note the unusual embossed area of visor.

The seam of the steel top makes the slope of the rain gutters far more pronounced.

The stainless steel radiator shell on this vehicle is an accessory.

A locking handle, with an integral keylock, is placed on the curbside door.

1928

The designation "AA" was reserved for the heavy-duty Model A truck line which was built on a 131½" wheelbase, well over two feet longer than the conventional 103½" listed for the passenger cars and "light duty" commercial vehicles. In addition to this stake bed truck, there was also available a panel truck on this same extended wheelbase chassis.

While the other vehicles in the commercial line such as the Station Wagons, the Pick-Ups, and the light delivery and express cars employed the same style of rear end as the passenger cars, the extended chassis models used either a heavy-duty bevel gear rear end or a worm drive.

At first, the engines built for this application were designated with the letters "AA" before their serial numbers to designate the use of a heavy-duty clutch spring, but after February of 1928 this practice was abandoned in favor of the more common "A" designation as all engines were thereafter built with the same clutch.

1928 Type 188-A Stake Bed Truck   *Mr. Max Herman, Flintridge, California*

In addition to this stake body, an enclosed panel delivery model was also available.

Built in April of 1928, this vehicle has many early features including the single brake system.

Headlights, tail light, and radiator shell are all painted black.

Oversized, heavy-duty, 650:20 tires are installed on split-rim early wheels.

With the introduction of the dual-brake system, these modified disc-type wheels became standard.

These early AR truck wheels, although similar, are not the same as those used on passenger cars.

A leather-covered visor conceals a hand-operated windshield wiper. The rear-view mirror is a standard commercial type.

Commercial vehicles have a radiator medallion with the Ford script in black, not the passenger-style blue enamel.

The appearance of the front end is identical with that of the lighter-duty commercial vehicles which are built on the shorter wheelbase chassis. The motometer is an accessory.

No inside rear-view mirror is furnished. An outside-mounted mirror is provided to clear the load. Early nickeled knob inside door latches are provided.

A red rubber steering wheel appears in this vehicle.

With the single-brake system still intact, the hand brake lever is on the left side of the cab.

Steel running boards with no rubber covering are used. Door panels are cardboard; seats are artificial leather.

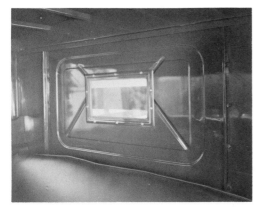

An embossed frame in the rear panel of
the cab holds the window glass.

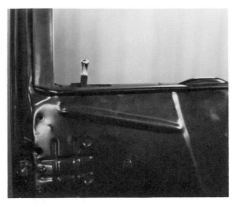

There are no outside door handles.
The latch is released by this through-
the-door handle similar to those
used on early passenger open cars.

The interior is plain and functional.
A rubber floor mat is provided.

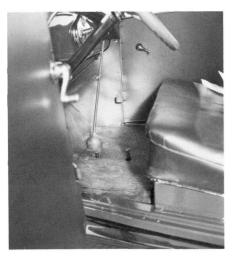

Two foot pedals work through a
linkage to control an optional
two-speed drive shaft.

The large 650:20 tires emphasise the hefty nature of the long wheelbase truck.

The body is sprung on extra-heavy springs placed laterally rather than across the vehicle as on passenger cars.

An idler arm operates to position the brake rod for maximum pull.

An accessory two-speed gear box called a "Dual High" unit is mounted behind the conventional transmission at the front of the drive shaft. Connected through a series of cables and pulleys to two footpedals on the floor of the cab for control, (page 286), this unit serves to double the number of rear-end gear ratios available. Consequently, this early truck has six speeds forward and two in reverse.

The better-known four-speed truck transmission did not become available until the late summer of 1929.

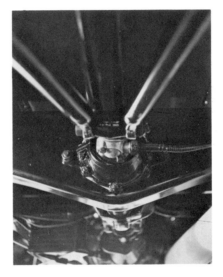

The truck spare wheel is mounted under the rear of the bed.

With the bed removed, the heavy wooden stringers on which it is mounted are exposed.

The worm and segment rear end drive provides more torque than does the ring and pinion. On the other hand, the high speed characteristics of the worm drive include excessive noise. Trucks, generally built for heavy hauling at low speeds, were therefore more frequently built with the worm drive rear end.

The worm gear rear end was available in ratios of both 7.25:1 and 5.17:1. It was discontinued in 1929.

The ring and pinion gear rear end was initially available in ratios of both 7.16:1 and 5.11:1. It was offered exclusively in 1930-31 and then had ratios of 6.6:1 and 5.14:1. Note the accessory dual rear wheels which are employed to improve traction and reduce tire loading.

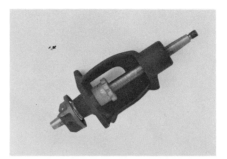

The packing nut on the Model A water pump was brass in 1928-29, and cadmium- or zinc-plated steel in 1930-31.

The new four cylinder engine introduced with the Model A was truly an improvement over the earlier, but similar, Model T. Rated at 40 horsepower, twice that of the Model T, its overall size and weight was only slightly more.

The Model A engine featured a water pump, an oil pump and a pressure lubrication system, and a crankshaft with main bearings 3/8" and rod bearings 1/4" larger than the sensitive Model T crankshaft. The engine was a masterpiece of evolutionary growth. Indeed, the last fifteen percent of the increase of Hp is said to have been as much the result of the use of larger valves and a more efficient carburetor as it was from the use of pistons one eighth of an inch larger in diameter.

A significant change within the engine occurred in late 1928 when the original five-bearing camshaft was replaced with a three-bearing shaft and the block altered accordingly.

SPECIFICATIONS:

Four cylinder, "L" head, cast en bloc
Piston displacement, 200.5 cubic inches
Bore: 3 7/8 inches, Stroke: 4 1/4 inches
Horsepower rating: 24.03 SAE, Brake
    horsepower 40 at 2200 RPM

1929 Canadian-built right-hand drive Model A engine

CLEARANCES AND LIMITS USED IN ASSEMBLY OF MODEL "A" ENGINES

Size of Parts

Diameter of pistons................3.8745
Diameter of cylinder bore..........3.876
Diameter of crankshaft main bearings.1.624
Diameter of crankshaft pin bearings..1.499
Diameter of camshaft bearings.......1.560

Shims .002 thick are placed between all main and connecting rod bearings after burnishing. This is for oil clearance.

Clearances

Piston clearance in cylinders—.002 maximum.
Piston ring gap—Lower ring .008 to .010.
Piston ring gap—Center ring .010 to .012.
Piston ring gap—Upper ring .012 to .015.
Ring groove clearance .001".
Piston pins are fitted in connecting rod bushings .0003 maximum
Pin assembled in piston .0002 to .0005 shrink fit.
Pistons are assembled with split side of skirt towards left side of engine.
Connecting rod side play at lower end of rod .008 to .012.
Clearance between piston bosses at upper end .040 to .053.
Connecting rod fitted to crankshaft .001" clearance.
Connecting rods are installed with oil dips towards camshaft.
Crankshaft end play .002 to .004.
Main bearing clearance .001.
Camshaft bearing clearance .003 maximum.
Camshaft end play taken up by tension of spring in front cover—Tension of spring, approximately 35 lbs.
Clearance between valves and push rods .010 to .013.
Exhaust valves fitted in valve guides .002 clearance.
Intake valves fitted in valve guides .001 to .0015.
Valve lift .287.
Push rod clearance .0015.
Time gear backlash .004".
End play of water pump shaft .006 to .010.
Flywheel eccentricity and wobble (indicator reading) after mounting flywheel on C/S—not more than .005.
Breaker point gap .018 to .022.
Spark plug gap .035.
Free movement or end play in clutch pedal, 1" minimum.

An oil pump is placed within the crankcase. This pump is driven by a geared shaft which in turn is driven by a gear on the camshaft. The intermediate shaft is inserted through the block and head, and turns the distributor above.

This two-bladed propellor-type fan was used throughout Model A production.

1930 Model A Ford engine

The lighter original Abel starter, perhaps the result of using Model T type components, proved to be too light for Model A, and was replaced in late 1928 with the Bendix unit shown on the right. With a heavier output shaft, the new Bendix unit was also furnished as a retrofit kit for those engines using the lighter Abel starter.

All Model A carburetors were furnished by either Zenith or Holley. Several significant obvious changes were made during production. Among these were the addition, in April of 1928, of a lower leg to the choke lever (to permit choking from the front while cranking), and the relocation of the sediment bowl to the inlet of the carburetor in May of 1931.

The Powerhouse generator on the far left is a five-brush design which was used into late 1928 and then replaced with the more familiar three-brush style shown on the near right. Only minor changes were then made in it including the elimination of the locking screw on the adjustable third brush and the addition of oil fittings in the early part of 1930.

1931 Model A Ford engine

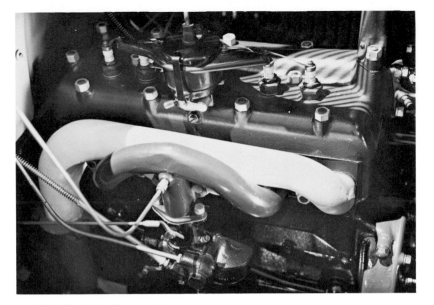

1931 Model A Ford engine

Early in 1932, concurrent with the introduction of the V-8 engine and the new Model 18 body styles, Ford introduced the "improved 4-cylinder" engine. Mounted on rubber mounts to reduce noise and vibration, it was claimed that the Model B engine would develop 50 horsepower, an increase of 25% over Model A. A high compression head with improved combustion chambers and modified valve ports accounted for most of this.

The Model B engine was designed to be installed in the 1932 type bodies (see THE V-8 AFFAIR, an illustrated history of the pre-war Ford V-8) which had their fuel tanks located at the rear and thus required a fuel pump to deliver the gasoline to the carburetor. Thus, when the higher-performance engine is to be installed in a Model A chassis as a retrofit, it becomes necessary to use a blanking plate over the fuel pump mounting boss (see photo below) just ahead of the carburetor.

1932 Model B Ford engine installed in a Model A

The water outlet casting and water pump as used on the Model B head are identical to the same area of the Model A. A letter "B" is cast into the head between cylinders 2 & 3.

1932 Model B Ford engine installed in a Model A

With the introduction of the 1933 models, Ford announced the Model C engine, the last upward revision of this versatile and reliable four cylinder engine, which was then abandoned in 1934. Essentially the same as the Model B engine, the fundamental difference was in the use of a completely counter-balanced crankshaft, a larger water pump, and a head that permitted better cooling.

1933 Model C Ford engine installed in a Model A

The water pump on this Model C engine is now mounted with three bolts rather than four, and the water outlet has been changed. Note blanking plate over fuel pump mount.

The letter "C" is cast into the head between cylinders 2 & 3. A fuel pump brings the gasoline from the rear-mounted tank.

1933 Type 700 Tudor sedan with Model C four cylinder engine

ENGINE NUMBERS AND DATING

Although engines *do* bear a number, and this can be used to accurately determine the date of manufacture *of the engine*, there is no certain correlation between that date and the date of assembly of the automobile in which it was used. While true that the engine number became the car's serial number as well, there may well have been great delays in the installation of a finished engine into an automobile.

From late in 1928, through the summer of 1929, the assembly date was stamped into the lower left corner of the fuel tank. This is the only reliable key to the assembly date.

OLD
☆A1234567890☆

NEW
☆A I234567890☆

Early in 1931, the design of the engine number stamps was changed to eliminate previous confusion.

For their first three years of production, Ford records indicate an excess of engine production over vehicle production of approximately 70,000 units per year. Then, in 1931, there appears to have been almost 140,000 more vehicles than engines produced, substantially reducing engine inventory. Nevertheless, Model A production ended with a substantial number of assembled engines ready, but unused.

MODEL A ENGINE NUMBERS

1927

October 20, 1928	1	137
November	138	971
December	972	5275

1928

January	5276	17251
February	17252	36016
March	36017	67700
April	67701	109740
May	109741	165726
June	165727	224276
July	224277	295707
August	295708	384867
September	384868	473012
October	473013	585696
November	585697	697829
December	697830	810122

1929

January	. . . . . .	810123	 983136
February	. . . . . .	983137	 1127171
March	. . . . . .	1127172	 1298827
April	. . . . . .	1298828	 1478647
May	. . . . . .	1478648	 1663401
June	. . . . . .	1663402	 1854831
July	. . . . . .	1854832	 2045422
August	. . . . . .	2045423	 2243920
September	. . . . . .	2243921	 2396932
October	. . . . . .	2396933	 2571781
November	. . . . . .	2571782	 2678140
December	. . . . . .	2678141	 2742695

1930

January	. . . . . .	2742696	 2826649
February	. . . . . .	2826650	 2940776
March	. . . . . .	2940777	 3114465
April	. . . . . .	3114466	 3304703
May	. . . . . .	3304704	 3509306
June	. . . . . .	3509307	 3702547
July	. . . . . .	3702548	 3771362
August	. . . . . .	3771363	 3883888
September	. . . . . .	3883889	 4005973
October	. . . . . .	4005974	 4093995
November	. . . . . .	4093996	 4177733
December	. . . . . .	4177734	 4237500

1931

January	. . . . . .	4237501	 4310300
February	. . . . . .	4310301	 4393627
March	. . . . . .	4393628	 4520831
April	. . . . . .	4520832	 4611921
May	. . . . . .	4611922	 4695999
June	. . . . . .	4696000	 4746730
July	. . . . . .	4746731	 4777282
August	. . . . . .		. . . . . .
September	. . . . . .	4777283	 4824809
October	. . . . . .	4824810	 4826746
November	. . . . . .	4826747	 4830806
December	. . . . . .		. . . . . .

1932

January	. . . . . .	4830807	 4842983
February	. . . . . .	4842984	 4846691
March	. . . . . .	4846692	 4849340

In general, a tool kit with the items listed below was furnished with each Model A delivered. In addition, there were many accessory items of great popularity including the lamp bulb kit, the tire patch kit, and the tire pressure gage shown here. Tools, quite naturally, varied from time to time, but in general, the standard complement, contained in a snap pouch made from surplus top materials were:

Adjustable wrench	two tire irons
two open end wrenches	jack
pliers	grease gun
screwdriver	tire pump
combination spark plug-	
and head bolt wrench	
Instruction book	

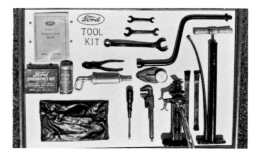

Prior to April of 1928, all tools were marked with the Ford script, but after that, only those actually manufactured by Ford were so marked. After March of 1929, the tool pouch shown was replaced with one with a single snap-fastened lip at the narrow end.

A dual-filament bulb, installed in a receptacle in a nickel-plated parabolic housing, was used on the headlamps of the 1928 Model A. An adjusting screw at the back of the shell could be turned to move the bulb housing as required to provide the most efficient focus. The entire light was rotated as necessary to correct aim.

The simple pattern of straight, vertical, flutes is typical for 1928. The Ford script appears at the bottom.

The early (1928) drum type taillamp is made of brass and nickel plated. The legend on the top is DUOLIGHT, and the red glass lens conceals a dual filament stop- and tail-light.

Headlights now bear the name TWO-LITE, and are furnished with a two-bulb reflector. A 15 candle-power bulb provides the parking light, and a dual-filament 32-32 cp bulb is the driving light.

Ford script appears in the bottom of the lens.

The lens pattern has been changed, possibly to produce a better beam.

Cowl lamps, introduced this year on the Town Sedan and the Convertible Cabriolet, are cup-shaped, and supported on long arms. When installed, the dual-bulb reflector in the headlamp is replaced with a single-bulb reflector. The lighting switch at the base of the steering column was modified in 1929 to provide, in addition to DIM and BRIGHT, an added PARK circuit control of these lamps or the small bulb in the headlight.

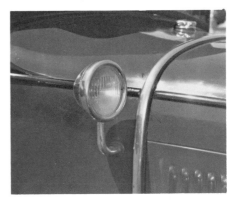

The typical 1929 tail light is this cup-shaped, nickel-plated brass light. The legend on the top is DUOLAMP.

A new alloy "rustless" (stainless) steel was introduced in 1930, and used extensively. The headlamps were not overlooked, and the result was these beautiful lights manufactured by Adlake and stamped TWOLITE. They are highly buffed and polished to an attractive shine.

More hemispheric than parabolic, these new lights use the same lens as the 1929 style and the Ford script continues to appear at the bottom of the lens.

The cowl lights are also made of rustless steel, but are now mounted on far more attractive brackets.

The tail light is also made of rustless steel, but is quite similar in appearance to the 1929 style. When illuminated by the dual-filament bulb, the lens shows red for the marker light function, but displays a distinctive amber-red for STOP.

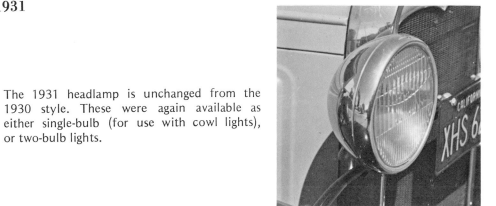

The 1931 headlamp is unchanged from the 1930 style. These were again available as either single-bulb (for use with cowl lights), or two-bulb lights.

The attractive cowl lamps are unchanged from the 1930 style.

As with the other lights, the tail lights were unchanged.

The Commercial line generally employed the same type of lamp as those on the passenger cars except that the rear was painted black. All of these lamps used a dual bulb reflector after 1929 as cowl lights were not normally furnished on commercial vehicles. The use of an "earlier" style light on a commercial vehicle is not unusual as it was in the truck line that Ford disposed of obsoleted passenger car items.

The Commercial tail light was also painted black to match the headlamps. Earlier, in 1928-29, a black-painted drum-type tail lamp similar to that on the passenger cars was used.

Two types of accessories can be recognized. One is the type that adds to the comfort, the riding pleasure, the convenience, or the safety of the driver. The other, less obvious, but equally non-standard, is the "cosmetic" accessory.

Model A existed in a period of time not too long after the exit of the family horse, and sometimes found itself the object of cosmetic or "dress-up" items of accessory that in truth had little whatever to do with aiding or improving the operation. Strangely, it seems that now, in 1972, similarly affectionate Model A restorers are increasingly directing their efforts towards the addition of some of these cosmetic accessories to their cars, and the day may not be too long distant when the lowly raccoon tail may make its return to the roadster windshield stanchions.

Among the most popular of all Model A accessories is the welled fender. Initially introduced as a commercial (truck) fender, and provided in order to improve access to the working rear body, the left-hand fender *did*, in fact, add a sporty look to the passenger car, and eventually became standard on the 1930 Deluxe Phaetons and Roadsters. Much earlier, in May of 1928, Ford announced the availability of both right- and left-hand welled fenders and thus they *were* optional extra cost equipment from then on. Curiously, the right-hand welled fender *did* have a non-cosmetic justification; Contractors, long accustomed to carrying ladders on their vehicles, found the left-side mounted wheel in their way!

Another "cosmetic" accessory, this time somewhat anachronistic since it did not become popular on Fords until the mid-thirties, is the white sidewall tire. While presumably dressing up the appearance, these added nothing to comfort, safety, or performance.

This lipped visor for the headlights added to the appearance, and to some degree, the function of the lights. It is today a rare accessory.

Most rare of all the accessories may be this hood with three louvred doors on each side. Originally sold as two side panels only, to be attached to an existing hood, the panels contain three individually adjustable ventilating doors which can be opened to increase cooling air flow.

A bud vase warms the interior of this Tudor.

Folding window awnings, similar to those offered by Sears Roebuck in 1927, protrude from the window.

Perhaps the most famous of all Model A cosmetic accessories is the quail radiator cap ornament. Greatly popular for its sculptured good looks, it aided appearance, but did little else.

The Motometer served a practical function in addition to being decorative. It contained a thermometer on the rear side which advised the driver of the radiator condition.

An accessory for the accessory is this example of the radiator Moto-wings ornament installed beneath the Motometer.

An early Ford accessory was a welled fender lock (shown here on a 1930 wheel) which was said to be effective in reducing theft.

This rear-mounted spare wheel lock not only protected the wheel, but also locked the tire to the wheel.

Available from Ford by June of 1930, was this handsome metal spare wheel cover with a painted faceplate and chromed outer ring. Optionally available with a painted outer ring, it is made for the 19" wheels and does not correctly fit the larger ones. After April of 1931 a similar all-black version was offered.

First offered by Ford about the end of 1927, this spare tire cover is made of top material and bears the Ford script.

A most popular safety accessory is the Rocky Mountain Brake which is a finned band pressed onto the brake drums. These cool the brakes by radiating heat and lessen brake fade.

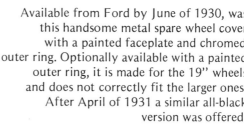

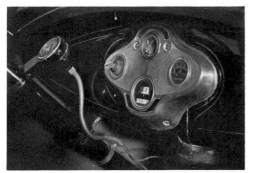

This water temperature guage is a practical accessory which is installed on the steering column. The lower end is connected to a hollow bolt which replaces a head stud.

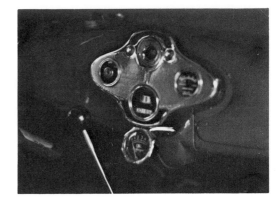

Oil pressure can be read on this Ford accessory guage designed to be fastened under the standard instrument panel.

Truly a "cosmetic" accessory is this jeweled panel light.

Perhaps the "daddy" of them all is this dress-up accessory instrument panel which is fastened directly over the original and which adds two guages for reading water temperature and oil pressure.

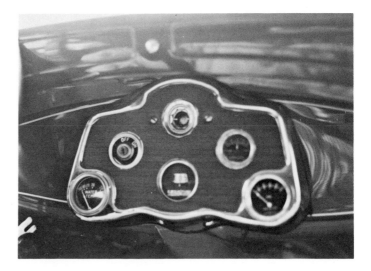

This original New Haven clock has a round, two-tone, face. The works are wound by pulling the string below the clock.

Windwings have been established through our text as either standard issue or as accessories as applicable. Another example of the cosmetic accessory though is the etched pattern.

Stone guards are an accessory which may protect a radiator from flying debris. This one is provided with an accessory crank hole cover.

Accessory step plates may be argued to provide better footing for entering passengers, or may be purely "cosmetic".

This accessory crankcase breather combines a screened fume vent and an easily opened non-spill filler tube.

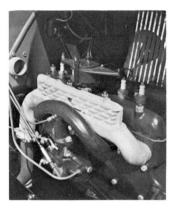

The manifold hot air heater is shown here. The finned exhaust manifold is installed in place of the conventional one, and a cast iron duct fitted over it to direct the incoming air over the heated fins and on into the passenger compartment through a hole in the firewall. Dangerous if the manifold should leak exhaust fumes into the passenger compartment, this type of heater soon lost favor.

An air cleaner is attached to the air intake of the carburetor and filters incoming air.

A more common crankcase breather is this one which directs the fumes down and beneath the car to be left behind by the moving vehicle.

The Luggage Carrier Rack was offered by Ford early in 1929. Constructed of steel, finished in black enamel, it was attractive and added to the appearance of the car as well as providing a practical storage and carrying rack.

Introduced at about the same time was this quality trunk designed to be carried on the Ford rack. Constructed of basswood, it had an extruded metal lip with a rubber gasket to provide a weathertight seal, and customarily was furnished with two cowhide straps for security.

The 1930-31 Deluxe cars justified a more elaborate luggage carrier than had previously been available, and this new design was brought out by Ford. Made of chromed steel, and with varnished wood strips for added effect, this rack was generally installed with a full-width rear bumper for added protection. This, however, disappeared when the rack was lowered for use.

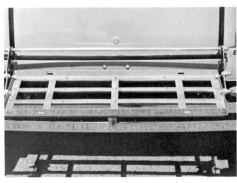

An accessory metal trunk shown mounted here on the Convertible Sedan with the full width rear bumper, shows how extenders are used to displace the bumper into a position where it protects the trunk.

A non-Ford low-profile accessory
trunk enhances the rear of a Roadster.

Extenders displace the spare wheel mounting
to allow a space for the accessory trunk.

A contoured Ford trunk
fits nicely to the back
of a Fordor.

The Kari-Kleen accessory trunk also
provided for a rear-mounted spare
and included extender brackets
for the rear bumpers.

A less common accessory is this
dual spare wheel mount.

The center bumper bar is a popular accessory
which protects the rear-mounted spare.

This Ford accessory rack contains three cans for oil, water, and gasoline, on the running board. Latching the cover secures the cans by locking their necks into a recess in the cover.

The Model A Sportlight, introduced late in 1928, was an adjustable accessory light. Mounting brackets for closed cars differed from this Roadster mount.

nd so it seems to be over. Henry's Lady has received affection, and in return has given of herself all that it was possible to give. Reliable and sturdy to the end, Model A dragged on into a new era, one in which her drabness, her lack of competitive power and speed, and her plainness doomed her. For the era of major automotive growth had not yet ended with the Model A. Indeed, as early as the Fall of 1930, rumors were raging about a *new* "new Ford", and the factory engaged in denying these rumors even as it had those of the coming of the Model A only three years earlier.

s it wore out, the Model A, having nothing left to give, stopped giving and retreated to hidden corners to await the attention of a new generation, an attention to which it has now become heir. Henry's Lady has again come of age. No longer the looked-down-upon faithful worker, reliable but unacceptable, Cinderella has emerged, repleat with charm, revitalized by renovation, and prepared again to meet her suitors.

In the cities, on the farms, around the towns of this world are still the remains of some four million Model A Fords. Although rapidly dwindling in number, there *are* those which still do exist. Resolve to find *yours* now before it's gone, and really *know* Henry's Lady!

1928-1929

FORD PASSENGER, COMMERCIAL AND TRUCK MODELS

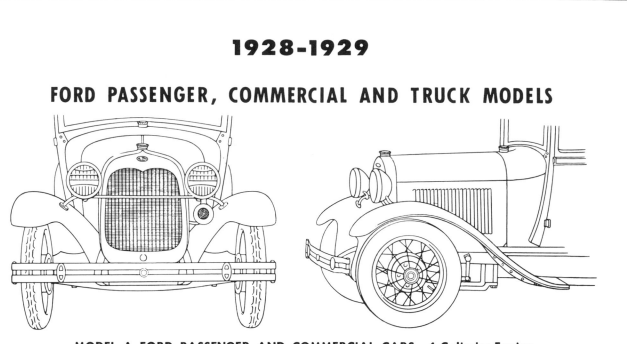

MODEL A FORD PASSENGER AND COMMERCIAL CARS—4 Cylinder Engine
(103½" Wheelbase)

MODEL AA FORD TRUCK—4 Cylinder Engine
(131½" Wheelbase)

BODY TYPE	NAME	YEAR	BODY TYPE	NAME	YEAR
			PASSENGER		
35-A	Phaeton (Std.)	1928-29	60-C	Fordor Sedan (steel back) (Briggs)	1929
40-A	Roadster (Std.)	1928-29	68-A	Cabriolet	1929
45-A	Coupe (Std.)	1928-29	140-A	Town Car	1928-29
49-A	Coupe (Special)	1928-29	150-A	Station Wagon	1928-29
50-A	Coupe (Sport)	1928-29	155-A	Town Sedan (Murray)	1929
54-A	Coupe (Business)	1928-29	155-B	Town Sedan (Briggs)	1929
55-A	Tudor Sedan	1928-29	165-A	Fordor Sedan (Std.) (Murray)	1929
60-A	Fordor Sedan (leather back—seal brown top) (Briggs)	1928-29	165-B	Fordor Sedan (Std.) (Briggs)	1929
60-B	Fordor Sedan (leather back—black top) (Briggs)	1929	170-A	Fordor Sedan (Std.) (2 Window)	1929
			170-B	Fordor Sedan (Dlx.) (2 Window)	1929
			COMMERCIAL AND TRUCKS		
76-A	Cab (Open)	1928-29	88-A	Platform	1928-29
78-A	Pickup	1928-29	89-A	Express	1928-29
79-A	Panel Delivery (103½" Wheelbase)	1928-29	130-A	De Luxe Delivery	1928-29
82-A	Cab (Closed)	1928-29	135-A	Taxicab	1928-29
85-A	Panel Delivery (131½" Wheelbase)	1928-29	188-A	Stake (131½" Wheelbase)	1928-29

1930

FORD PASSENGER, COMMERCIAL AND TRUCK MODELS

MODEL A FORD PASSENGER CAR
4 Cylinder Engine (103½" Wheelbase)

MODEL AA FORD TRUCK
4 Cylinder Engine (131½" and 157" Wheelbase)

MODEL A FORD COMMERCIAL—4 Cylinder Engine
(103½" Wheelbase)

BODY TYPE	NAME	BODY TYPE	NAME
	PASSENGER		
35-B	Phaeton (Standard)	155-C	Town Sedan (Murray)
40-B	Roadster (Standard)	155-D	Town Sedan (Briggs)
40-B	Roadster (De Luxe)	165-C	Fordor Sedan (Standard) (Murray)
45-B	Coupe (Standard)	165-D	Fordor Sedan (Standard) (Briggs)
45-B	Coupe (De Luxe)	170-B	Fordor Sedan (Standard) (2 Window)
50-B	Coupe (Sport)	170-B	Fordor Sedan (De Luxe) (2 Window)
55-B	Tudor Sedan	180-A	Phaeton (De Luxe)
68-B	Cabriolet	190-A	Victoria
	COMMERCIAL AND TRUCK		
76-A	Cab (Open)	202-A	Gravity dump body assembly (Anthony)
76-B	Cab (Open)	203-A	Garbage body with heavy hydraulic hoist (2 cu. yd. capacity) (Galion)
78-A	Pickup		
79-A	"A" Panel Delivery	203-B	Garbage body with heavy hydraulic hoist (2 cu. yd. capacity) (Wood)
79-B	"A" Panel Delivery		
82-A	Cab (Closed)	203-C	Garbage body with heavy hydraulic hoist (3 cu. yd. capacity) (Galion)
82-B	Cab (Closed)		
85-A	"A" Panel Delivery	203-D	Garbage body with heavy hydraulic hoist (3 cu. yd. capacity) (Wood)
85-B	"AA" Panel Delivery		
88-A	Platform	204-A	Dump body with light hydraulic hoist (1½ cu. yd. capacity) (Galion)
89-A	Express		
130-A	De Luxe Delivery	204-B	Dump body with light hydraulic hoist (1½ cu. yd. capacity) (Wood)
130-B	De Luxe Delivery (drop floor)		
130-B	De Luxe Delivery (Standard)	205-A	Hi-Lift Hydraulic Coal Body (72 cu. ft.) (Wood)
150-B	Station Wagon	206-A	Dump body with Rotary power hoist (Anthony)
185-A	Platform (157" Wheelbase)	207-B	Combined dump and coal body with high sides and end gate with chute opening and swinging partition with heavy hydraulic hoist (1½ cu. yd. capacity) (120 cu. ft. with top boards)
186-A	Stake (157" Wheelbase)		
188-A	Stake (131½" Wheelbase)		
200-A	Hand hoist dump body assembly (Anthony)		
201-A	Coal body, with heavy hydraulic hoist and end gate with chute (less swinging partition) (75 cu. ft.) (Galion)	208-A	Dump body with heavy hydraulic hoist (1½ cu. yd. capacity) (Galion)
201-B	Coal body with heavy duty hydraulic hoist, swinging partition and end gate with chute (high end) (75 cu. ft. or 120 cu. ft. with sides) (Wood)	208-B	Dump body with heavy hydraulic hoist (1½ cu. yd. capacity) (Wood)
		225-A	"A" Panel Delivery (with drop floor)
201-C	Coal body with heavy duty hydraulic hoist and end gate with chute (less swinging partition) (75 cu. ft.) (Wood)	236-A	Light hydraulic hoist and body understructure (Galion)
		237-A	Heavy hydraulic hoist and body understructure (Galion)

1931

FORD PASSENGER CAR MODELS

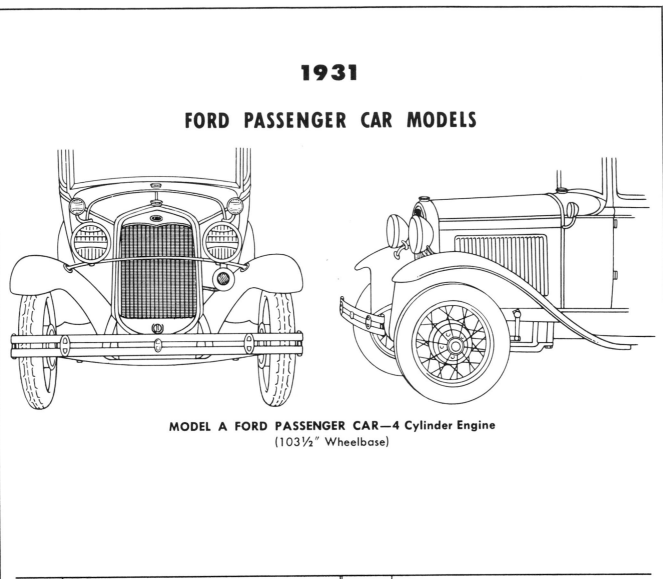

MODEL A FORD PASSENGER CAR—4 Cylinder Engine
(103½" Wheelbase)

BODY TYPE	NAME	BODY TYPE	NAME
35-B	Phaeton (Standard)	155-C	Town Sedan (Murray)
40-B	Roadster (Standard)	155-D	Town Sedan (Briggs)
40-B	Roadster (De Luxe)	160-A	Fordor Sedan (Standard)
45-B	Coupe (Standard)	160-B	Town Sedan
45-B	Coupe (De Luxe)	160-C	Fordor Sedan (De Luxe)
50-B	Coupe (Sport)	165-C	Fordor Sedan (Standard) (Murray)
55-B	Tudor Sedan	5-D	Fordor Sedan (Standard) (Briggs)
68-B	Cabriolet	170-B	Fordor Sedan (De Luxe) (2 Window)
68-C	Cabriolet	180-A	Phaeton (De Luxe)
		190-A	Victoria

1931

FORD COMMERCIAL AND TRUCK MODELS

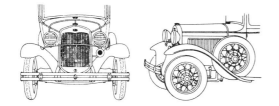

MODEL A FORD COMMERCIAL—4 Cylinder Engine
(103½" Wheelbase)

MODEL AA FORD TRUCK—4 Cylinder Engine
(131½" and 157" Wheelbase)

BODY TYPE	NAME	BODY TYPE	NAME
65-A	Canopy and Screens (Used with Type 78-B)	204-B	Dump body with light hydraulic hoist (1½ cu. yd. capacity) (Wood)
66-A	De Luxe Pickup	205-A	Hi-Lift Hydraulic Coal Body (72 cu. ft.) (Wood)
76-B	Cab (Open)	206-B	Dump body with mechanical hoist (1½ cu. yd. capacity) (Detwiller)
78-A	Pickup		
78-B	Pickup	207-B	Combined dump and coal body with high sides and end gate with chute opening and swinging partition (1½ cu. yd. capacity) (120 cu. ft. with top boards)
79-A	Panel Delivery (103½" Wheelbase)		
79-B	Panel Delivery (103½" Wheelbase)		
82-B	Cab (Closed)		
85-B	Panel Delivery (131½" Wheelbase)	208-A	Dump body with heavy hydraulic hoist (1½ cu. yd. capacity) (Galion)
130-B	De Luxe Delivery (Drop Floor)		
130-B	De Luxe Delivery (Standard)	208-B	Dump body with heavy hydraulic hoist (1½ cu. yd. capacity) (Wood)
150-B	Station Wagon		
185-B	Platform (157" Wheelbase)	210-A	"AA" Panel Delivery
186-B	Stake (157" Wheelbase)	225-A	"A" Panel Delivery (with drop floor)
187-A	Platform (131½" Wheelbase)	228-A	Stock Racks
189-A	Stake (131½" Wheelbase)	229-A	Service Car
195-A	Express Body (131½" Wheelbase)	236-A	Light hydraulic hoist and body understructure (Galion)
196-A	Canopy Top and Screens (For 195-A)		
197-A	Express Body (157" Wheelbase)	236-B	Light hydraulic hoist and body understructure (Wood)
198-A	Canopy Top and Screens (For 197-A)		
199-A	Ice Wagon	237-A	Heavy hydraulic hoist and body understructure (Galion)
200-B	Dump Body with hand hoist (1½ cu. yd. capacity) (Galion)		
		237-B	Heavy hydraulic hoist and body understructure (Wood)
201-A	Coal body with heavy hydraulic hoist and end gate with chute (less swinging partition) (75 cu. ft.) (Galion)		
		238-A	Stock Racks (157" Wheelbase)
		239-A	Meat Packers Express
		242-A	Heavy Duty Express Body (131½" Wheelbase)
201-B	Coal body with heavy duty hydraulic hoist, swinging partition and end gate with chute (high end) (75 cu. ft. or 120 cu. ft. with sides) (Wood)	244-A	Grain body with or without stock rack or grain side extensions) (157" Wheelbase)
		248-A	Grain body with or without stock rack or grain side extensions (131½" Wheelbase)
201-C	Coal body with heavy duty hydraulic hoist and end gate with chute (less swinging partition) (75 cu. ft.) (Wood)	255-A	Special Delivery (Natural Wood)
		270-A	Funeral Service
202-B	Gravity dump body (1½ cu. yd. capacity) (Wood)	275-A	Funeral Coach
203-A	Garbage body with heavy hydraulic hoist (2 cu. yd. capacity) (Galion)	280-A	Ambulance
		285-A	Police Patrol (De Luxe)
203-B	Garbage body with heavy hydraulic hoist (2 cu. yd. capacity) (Wood)	290-A	Police Patrol (Standard)
		295-A	Town Car Delivery
203-C	Garbage body with heavy hydraulic hoist (3 cu. yd. capacity) (Galion)	300-A	De Luxe Delivery
		315-A	Standrive
203-D	Garbage body with heavy hydraulic hoist (3 cu. yd. capacity) (Wood)	330-A	School and Passenger Bus
204-A	Dump body with light hydraulic hoist (1½ cu. yd. capacity) (Galion)	400-A	Convertible Sedan

MODEL A PASSENGER CAR BODY STYLES

By Type Number

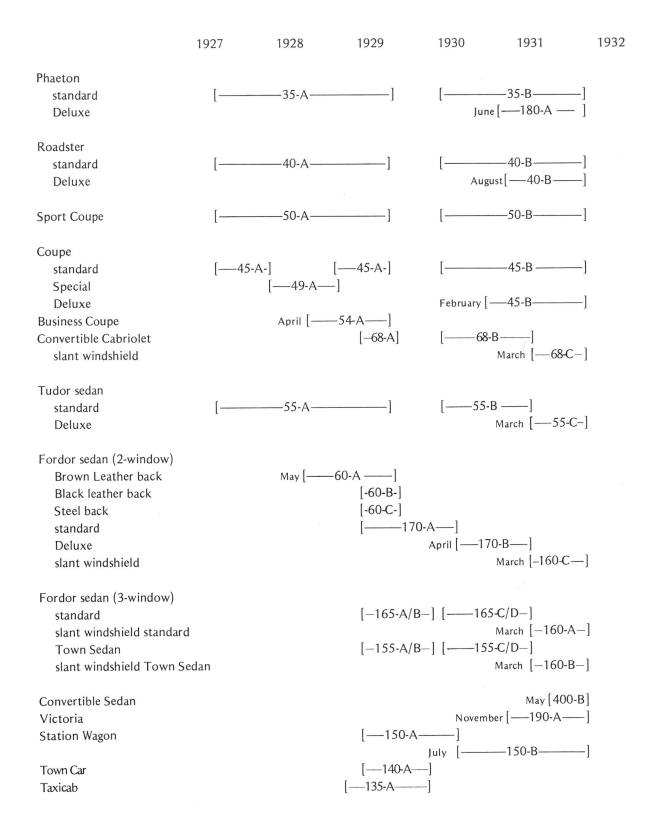

	1927	1928	1929	1930	1931	1932
Phaeton						
standard	[————35-A————]			[————35-B————]		
Deluxe				June [——180-A——]		
Roadster						
standard	[———— 40-A————]			[————40-B————]		
Deluxe				August [——40-B——]		
Sport Coupe	[————50-A————]			[————50-B————]		
Coupe						
standard	[—45-A-]	[—45-A-]		[————45-B————]		
Special		[—49-A—]				
Deluxe				February [——45-B————]		
Business Coupe		April [——54-A——]				
Convertible Cabriolet			[—68-A]	[——68-B——]		
slant windshield				March [——68-C—]		
Tudor sedan						
standard	[————55-A————]			[——55-B ——]		
Deluxe				March [——55-C–]		
Fordor sedan (2-window)						
Brown Leather back		May [——60-A ——]				
Black leather back		[-60-B-]				
Steel back		[-60-C-]				
standard		[————170-A——]				
Deluxe			April [——170-B——]			
slant windshield				March [–160-C—]		
Fordor sedan (3-window)						
standard		[–165-A/B–] [——165-C/D–]				
slant windshield standard				March [–160-A—]		
Town Sedan		[–155-A/B–] [——155-C/D–]				
slant windshield Town Sedan				March [–160-B—]		
Convertible Sedan				May [400-B]		
Victoria				November [——190-A——]		
Station Wagon			[——150-A————]			
			July [————150-B————]			
Town Car			[——140-A—]			
Taxicab			[——135-A——]			

MODEL A DOMESTIC PRODUCTION FIGURES

	1927	1928	1929	1930	1931	Totals
Phaeton						
standard	221	47,255	49,818	16,479	4,076	117,849
Deluxe				3,946	2,229	6,175
Roadster						
standard	269	81,937*	191,529	112,901	5,499	392,135
Deluxe				11,318	52,997	64,315
Sport Coupe	734	79,099	134,292	69,167	19,700	302,992
Coupe						
standard	629	70,784	178,982	226,027	79,816	556,238
Deluxe				28,937	23,067	52,004
Business Coupe		37,343	37,644			74,987
Convertible Cabriolet			16,421	25,868	11,801	54,090
Tudor						
Tudor						
standard	1,948	208,562	523,922	376,271	148,425	1,259,128
Deluxe					21,984	21,984
Fordor (2-window)						
standard		82,349	146,097	5,279		233,725
Deluxe				12,854	3,251	16,105
Fordor (three-window)						
standard			53,941	41,133	18,127	113,201
Town Sedan			84,970	104,935	55,469	245,374
Convertible Sedan					4,864	4,864
Victoria				6,306	33,906	40,212
Town Car		89	913	63		1,065
Station Wagon		5	4,954	3,510	2,848	11,317
Taxicab		264	4,576	10		4,850
Truck	286	63,229	156,433	159,341	103,561	482,850
Commercial Chassis	99	42,612	130,608	56,708	34,959	264,986
	4,186	713,528	1,715,100	1,261,053	626,579	4,320,446

* Of these, 51,807 were produced without rumble seat.

From the Ford Motor Company production figures for the years stated. Extracted and originally compiled by Mr. Leslie R. Henry in 1958 through the courtesy of the Ford Archives, and retabulated in 1972 by the Author.

Reprinted by permission of Leslie R. Henry in whose book Henry's Fabulous Model A they first appeared, and with the additional permission of Floyd Clymer Publications, Los Angeles, California, publishers of that manuscript.

MODEL A FORD CLUBS

Newcomers to the hobby of restoring the Model A will find that they may serve their own best interests by joining one of the several established Clubs already serving the hobby. In general, the ? Clubs offer excellent publications, heavily saturated with needed restoration data, and in addition, local Chapters to provide for such social contacts as Tours, Swap Meets, and interesting Meetings which offer an opportunity to meet others who share your interest.

There are countless such Clubs, many of them unaffiliated, and thus relatively local or regional in scope. In addition to the all-car Clubs such as the Antique Automobile Club of America, (Hershey, Pennsylvania), and the Horseless Carriage Club of America, (Downey, California), there are *two* strong, exclusively Model A Organizations. Their dues are nominal, their entrance requirements minimal, (actually, your interest in the Model A qualifies you), and their publications are superb. Readers are urged to contact them:

Model "A" Restorers Club, Inc.
Post Office Box 1930A
Dearborn, Michigan, 48121
Publication: *Model "A" News*

Model A Ford Club of America, Inc.
Box 2564
Pomona, California, 91766
Publication: *The Restorer*